Historical Cities of Delhi: Walks Using the Delhi Metro

By Siva Prasad Bose and Joy Bose

Contents

Other Books by Siva Prasad Bose

Dedication

This book is dedicated to the present, past and future residents of Delhi and the people who played a role in building the historical cities of Delhi.

Preface

———

Delhi is much more than just the capital of India. It is a city with an amazing history. So many times, it has been the major city or capital of India, from the earliest Mahabharata days to the Rajputs to the Delhi Sultanate to the Mughals to the British. Each time the new rulers left their mark on the city. As a result, now we have a Delhi which has the mark of at least seven or eight different historical cities, if not more.

In this book, we review the different historical cities of Delhi. We use the Delhi metro, which is currently probably the best developed metro in India, as the preferred means of transport to see the sights of the seven cities of Delhi. We hope that this short guide will help the reader the experience a little bit of what Delhi is all about, its people and its history.

This 2025 updated edition has been revised to reflect major recent developments in Delhi, including the inauguration of the new triangular Parliament building in May 2023, the renaming of Rajpath to Kartavya Path in September 2022, significant progress on Delhi Metro Phase 4 expansion, and updated practical information for visitors including ticket prices, transport options, and walking routes. A new Practical Visitor's Guide chapter and a Glossary of Key Terms have also been added.

In this book, we do not cover all the historical sites or attractions of Delhi, such as the many modern museums, markets and other attractions. Rather, we focus on the sites that form part of the historical cities of Delhi and those that are located within the historical boundaries of those cities.

This book was born out of many travels and exploratory walks made by the authors in Delhi, where they live.

Acknowledgements

In preparing this book, the authors would like to acknowledge help from many travel websites, that proved invaluable when they were personally exploring many of described sights, particularly Wikitravel and Wikivoyage.

Some of the images were taken from Wikimedia and are cited accordingly.

We also consulted the following books:

- Delhi: Its Monuments and History. Perceival Spear. Oxford University Press.
- Footprint India Handbook 2002. Robert and Roma Bradnock. Footprint Books.
- Delhi and its neighborhood. By Y D Sharma. Archeological Survey of India. 2002.
- *City of Djinns: A Year in Delhi.* William Dalrymple. Penguin Books. 1993.
- *The Last Mughal: The Fall of a Dynasty, Delhi 1857.* William Dalrymple. Bloomsbury. 2006.
- *Delhi: A Novel.* Khushwant Singh. Penguin Books. 1990.
- Delhi Metro Rail Corporation (DMRC) official website and maps: www.delhimetrorail.com[1]
- Archaeological Survey of India (ASI) official website: www.asi.nic.in[2]

---

1. http://www.delhimetrorail.com

2. http://www.asi.nic.in

Note: Unless indicated, photos of the historical sites (that are not taken from Wikimedia) were taken personally by the authors.

Chapter 1: Introduction to the Historical Cities of Delhi

Delhi truly befits the capital of an empire such as India. It holds a deep regard in the minds of Indians as the capital and has been so for centuries. Its strategic location, in the middle of the northern plains of India on the banks of the river Yamuna, further adds to its aura as the capital and a very important historical city.

Over the centuries past, Delhi has been the site of multiple kingdoms, in fact it has been called the "Graveyard of Dynasties" by Lord Curzon the British viceroy of India. The earliest historical remains found in Delhi are from the lower paleolithic age. But its recorded history reportedly spans from the Iron age, where it was the site of the Pandava capital Indraprastha from the Indian epic Mahabharata reportedly composed around 400 BC or even earlier. Remains from that era are found in today's Purana Qila, and some articles such as pottery from that age have been excavated. The Buddhist literature of the Mauryan period of 3rd century BC also mention the town of Indapatta, belonging to the Kuru kingdom or Kuru Rattha which was one of the sixteen Mahajanapadas of India at that time. Emperor Ashoka's rock and pillar edicts have also been found in and around Delhi.

In the medieval ages, Delhi became been the site of the Delhi sultanate after the defeat of Prithviraj Chauhan by Mohammed Ghori. The numerous tombs and graves of the dynasties of sultans and their nobles testify to its significance as the capital of the Delhi sultanate. The shrines or dargahs of Sufi saints such as Sheikh Nizamuddin Auliya, who were based in Delhi and did most of their activity there, are still revered holy places, now as it was then. Poets and cultural luminaries such as Amir Khusro, Mirza Ghalib and Abdur Rahim Khan e Khanum all made their home here. Then came the mighty Mughals, followed by the British.

The mid-17th century French travelers Bernier and Tavernier praised the magnificent architecture of Red Fort in the city of Delhi. The silk route, which was an important medieval trade route connecting central Asia and China, also passed through Delhi. The wealth and fame of Delhi also attracted its share of foreign invaders, notable among whom were Timur in the 14th century, and Nadir Shah and Ahmed Shah Abdali in the 18th century. Delhi also had a pivotal role to play in the great revolt of 1857, for it was here that the sepoys declared the Mughal emperor Bahadur Shah Zafar as their leader, and it was here that the British defeated the revolt and declared the end of Mughal rule. In 1911, Delhi was the site of the magnificent Delhi Durbar organized by the British, where it was made the new capital of British India in a ceremony attended by all the kings and princes of various parts of India, to pay homage to the British king who was acknowledged as emperor of India. After the British left, it became the capital of independent India and an important industrial center, now again growing and absorbing neighboring cities such as Gurgaon and Noida on its way to becoming one of India's important IT hubs.

Figure: Delhi during the rains. AI generated art by Midjourney AI

Figure: Scene from the crowded markets of Bazars of Delhi. AI generated art by Midjourney AI

Figure: Chandni Chowk market in old Delhi. AI generated art by Dall E.

Delhi has seen numerous wars and change of governments. The centuries under the Delhi sultanate before the Mughals were an especially turbulent time for Delhi. Every time a new ruler came to the throne of Delhi, they sought it fit to leave their mark in terms of architecture, to build a new capital city in a fort, as it were. That is why Delhi has so many different cities and forts encompassing cities.

1.1 Names and locations of the different historical cities

The historical cities of Delhi, named in chronological order, are as follows:

- **Lal Kot or Qila Rai Pithora**: This was the fort city built and expanded by the Tomar and Chauhan rulers (possibly building up from even earlier constructions by Rajput and other rulers) before the conquest by Mohammed Ghori. It mainly consists of the remnants of a fort and located in South Delhi near Saket, including parts of Mahrauli.

- **Mehrauli**: This city is sometimes included in Lal Kot since the boundaries are overlapping. It includes the Mahrauli archeological park and the Qutub Minar complex. It was built by Qutubuddin Aibak after the Islamic conquest of Delhi, with Mohammed Ghori's victory over Prithviraj Chauhan in the 1192 second battle of Terain. The boundaries were further expanded by his successors including Iltutmish. It is located in South Delhi.

- **Siri**: This was the city built by the Khalji rulers that flourished in 14th century, and later expanded by Sher Shah Suri. It encompasses the Siri fort and surrounding areas. It is mainly located near Hauz Khas.

- **Tughlaqabad and Jahanpanah**: These were the cities built by the Tughlaq rulers in the 14th century. Tughlaqabad was started by Ghiyasuddin Tughlaq who built the Tughlaqabad fort, and whose tomb lies across the road from the fort. Jahanpanah was started by Mohammed Tughlaq in 1325 AD who combined the existing fortifications of Delhi, Siri and Tughlaqabad. It is located towards the South of Delhi near Panchsheel enclave and Malviya Nagar.

- **Firozabad**: This was founded by Firoze Tughlaq in 1354 AD. It includes parts of Hauz Khas and Feroze Shah Kotla fort.

- **Shergarh**: This was built by Sher Shah Suri and his successors in the 16th century, although its city limits and surrounding areas also include some ancient parts said to date from the time of the Pandavas. It includes Purana Qila and Humayun's tomb. This was built over the boundaries of **Dinpanah**, a city that was started by the Mughal emperor Humayun before he was defeated by Sher Shah Suri in battle.

- **Shahjahanabad**: This was the city built by the Mughal Emperor Shah Jahan and named after him. The red fort and surrounding areas were completed and inaugurated in 1648 AD. Shahjahanabad encompasses the Red Fort and Jama Masjid. It is located in the north in what is often called old Delhi.
- **New Delhi**: This was the city built by the British rulers of India as the new capital of British India when the capital was moved from Calcutta in 1911. It includes the magnificent Raj path connecting the India gate and Rashtrapati Bhavan, secretariat buildings, many of the central government offices such as Rail Bhavan, as well as markets such as Connaught place. After independence, New Delhi remained the capital of free India and many more government buildings were added.

Each of these historical cities can be the object of one or more separate walks. However, it must be noted that the boundaries of these cities can be overlapping. As each new ruler succeeded to the throne of Delhi, they often repaired and maintained the existing buildings or built new buildings within the boundaries of the earlier historical cities.

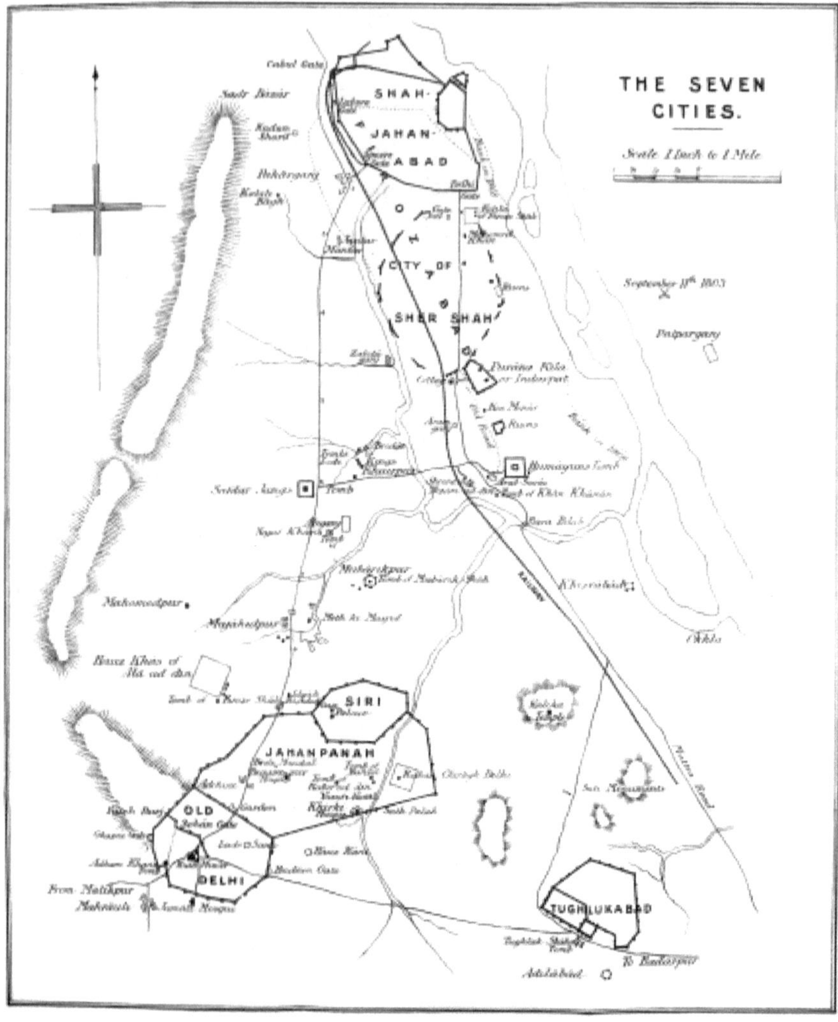

Figure: The Seven Cities of Delhi. Gordon Risley Hearn, Public domain, via Wikimedia Commons

The term Eight Cities of Delhi (sometimes called Seven Cities) is often used in notional terms to indicate the different historical capital cities built by different rulers of Delhi. However, in reality perhaps Delhi consists of more than seven or eight cities. With the recent expansion of Delhi to include Gurgaon and Noida as the NCR or National Capital Region, perhaps the IT hubs of Gurgaon and Noida, with their swanky offices, malls, and modern apartment complexes, could be construed as yet another of the cities of Delhi.

1.2 Best Time to Visit Delhi

Delhi has a semi-arid climate with four distinct seasons. Choosing the right time to visit makes a significant difference to the experience.

- **October to March (ideal):** Cool to mild weather with clear skies. December and January can be cold and foggy, especially in the mornings. This is the best period for walking tours.
- **April to June (hot):** Temperatures regularly exceed 40°C and can touch 45°C. Heatwaves are common. Outdoor walks should be planned for early morning only.
- **July to September (monsoon):** Heavy rain brings relief from heat but also flooding in low-lying areas. Many outdoor sites remain beautiful but can be muddy.

Tip: The Republic Day parade on 26 January along Kartavya Path (India Gate to Rashtrapati Bhavan) is a spectacular annual event. Book accommodation and Metro tickets well in advance if visiting around this date.

1.3 Buying tickets to the sites

Red Fort, Humayun's tomb and Qutub Minar complex are all separate UNESCO world heritage sites, so one needs to buy a ticket from Archeological Survey of India (ASI) ticket office located outside each of the sites. For most other historical sites as well, one needs to buy tickets from the ASI ticket booths.

Figure: Archeological Survey of India's QR code

Online ticketing has been significantly upgraded in recent years. Visitors can now book tickets for all 170+ ASI-protected monuments via the ASI payment portal at **https://asi.payumoney.com/** or through ONDC-enabled apps. A discount of approximately ₹5 (Indian nationals) or ₹50 (foreign nationals) is offered for online bookings versus walk-in cash payment.

Approximate Entry Fees (as of 2025):

Monument	Indian Nationals	Foreign Nationals
Red Fort (Lal Qila)	₹35	₹550
Qutub Minar Complex	₹35	₹550
Humayun's Tomb	₹35	₹550
Purana Qila	₹20	₹300
Hauz Khas Fort & Madrasa	₹20	₹300
Tughlaqabad Fort	₹20	₹300
Feroze Shah Kotla	₹20	₹300
Sunder Nursery	₹35	₹200
Safdarjung's Tomb	₹20	₹300
Lodi Gardens	Free	Free
Mehrauli Archaeological Park	Free	Free

Note: Fees are subject to revision. There is no additional charge for the Salimgarh Fort section of the Red Fort complex. Children under 15 are typically free at ASI sites.

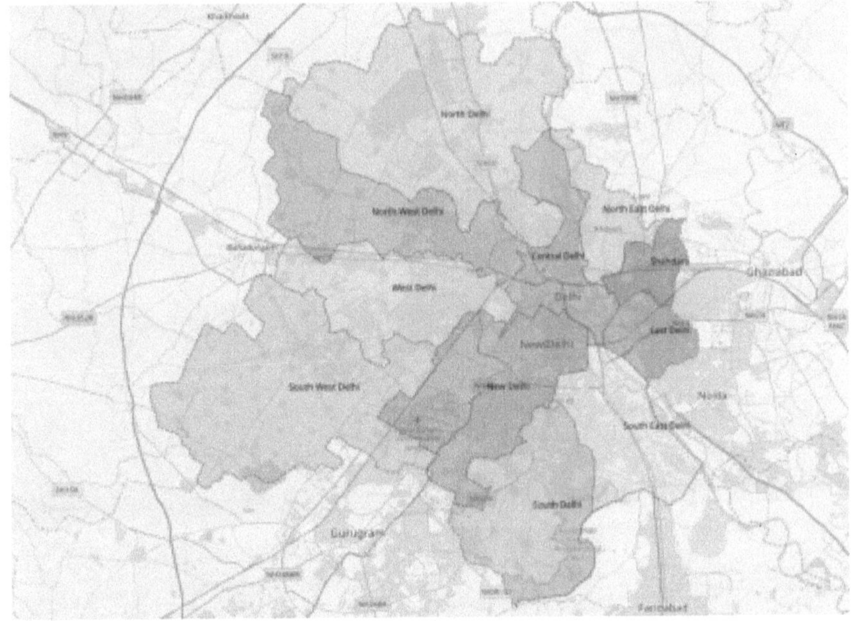

Figure: Modern day districts of Delhi. Heinz OSM, CC BY-SA 4.0 <https://creativecommons.org/licenses/by-sa/4.0>, via Wikimedia Commons

1.4 Conclusion

In this chapter, we have introduced the different historical cities of Delhi. We will do into details of each of the historical cities in the following chapters.

Chapter 2: Resources to Explore the Historical Cities of Delhi

In this chapter we introduce a few useful resources to help the reader to navigate Delhi and explore its historical cities.

2.1 Delhi metro

We start with the Delhi Metro. It is the preferred option for travel to historical sites in Delhi because of its flexibility and reliability. Most or all of the sites are located only a few km at most from the nearest metro station, making it convenient to use it to see all the sights, or to hire a cheap autorickshaw from the nearest metro station to travel to the exact locations of the sites.

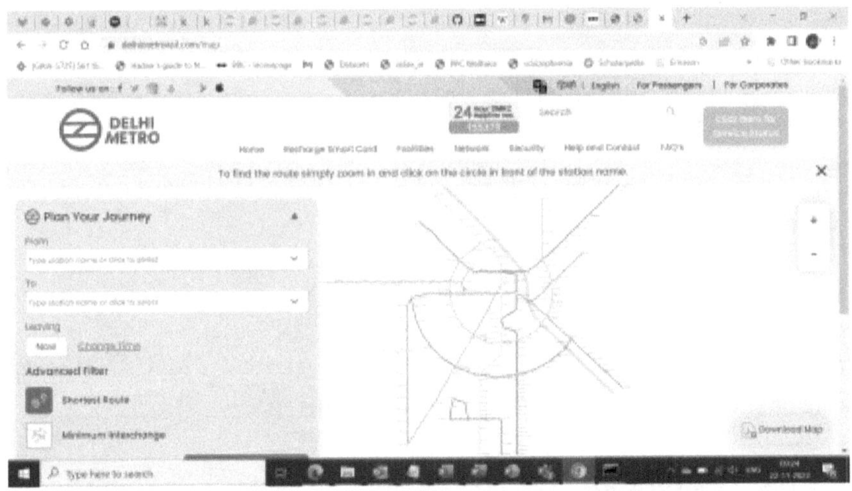

Figure: Delhi Metro Map, from the Delhi Metro Rail website

For travel using Delhi metro, it is usually better to get a Delhi metro smart card and recharge it periodically. This will save the visitor from having to queue and buy tickets for each metro journey.

Figure: Zoomed in Map of Central Delhi metro stations, from the Delhi Metro Rail website

Delhi Metro: Current Status (2025)

As of early 2025, the Delhi Metro Rail Corporation (DMRC) operates one of the world's largest urban metro systems:

- **Network size:** Over 395 km of track across 12 colour-coded corridors
- **Stations:** 289 stations, including elevated, underground, and at-grade
- **Daily ridership:** Approximately 5–6.5 million passenger

journeys on weekdays. A record single-day high of 7.86 million was recorded on 18 November 2024.

- **Operating hours:** Approximately 5:30 AM to 11:30 PM daily (varies by line)
- **Fares:** ₹10 to ₹60 per journey, based on distance. Smart card holders receive a 10% discount, with an additional 10% for off-peak travel.

Phase 4 Expansion (Under Construction)

Delhi Metro's Phase 4 is a major ongoing expansion project adding approximately 112 km of new lines across six corridors at an estimated cost of ₹24,949 crore:

- **Janakpuri West – RK Ashram Marg (Magenta Line extension):** The first 2.03 km section (Janakpuri West to Krishna Park Extension) was inaugurated by PM Modi on 5 January 2025, marking Phase 4's first operational stretch. The full 28.92 km corridor is expected by 2026.
- **Majlis Park – Maujpur (Pink Line extension):** This 12.3 km section was nearly complete as of early 2025, with trial runs underway. Expected to open by mid-2025, connecting northern Delhi localities including Sonia Vihar, Bhajanpura, Jagatpur Village, Jharoda Majra, and Burari.
- **Golden Line (Aerocity – Tughlakabad, Lines 10 and 11):** This entirely new 25.82 km mostly underground line with 16 stations will link IGI Airport Terminal 1 with Tughlakabad in South Delhi. It was specially re-routed in 2020 on ASI advice to avoid passing beneath the Qutub Minar and Mehrauli Archaeological Park. Completion targeted for 2026.
- **Lajpat Nagar – Saket G Block (Line 11 spur):** Approved

March 2024; 8.385 km. In planning stage.

- **Inderlok – Indraprastha (Green Line extension):** Approved March 2024; 12.377 km. In planning stage.
- **Rithala – Narela – Kundli:** Approved December 2024; 26.463 km Red Line extension into Haryana. Foundation stone laid January 2025.

Note for visitors: Phase 4 construction means some areas near active construction sites may have temporary road diversions. Always check the DMRC website (www.delhimetrorail.com[1]) or app for the latest route map before travel.

Smart Cards

For travel using the Delhi Metro, it is better to get a Delhi Metro smart card and recharge it periodically. This saves queuing to buy tokens for each journey and provides a 10% discount on all fares. Smart cards cost ₹200 (including ₹50 refundable deposit) and can be recharged at any metro station or via the DMRC app.

2.2 Alternative ways of exploring Delhi

Alternate ways of exploring Delhi include the following:

- Taking Delhi public buses to each of the sites. This is also a flexible and cheap option. The catch here is that one needs to know the bus numbers going to different locations. This can be combined with autorickshaws and other options.
- Hiring an Uber cab, Ola cab or other private taxi for the day. They would have fixed rates depending on the number of hours and distance travelled or sights seen.
- Hiring an autorickshaw to see the various sights of Delhi. The rates need to be negotiated in advance with the driver.

---

1. http://www.delhimetrorail.com

- Taking the Delhi tourism Hop On Hop Off (HOHO) bus or any of the private bus based tours available. The HOHO Delhi sightseeing bus tour starts from Saket metro station and has pick up points including INA, Shivaji Stadium and RK Ashram metro stations. Many of the private tours start from the Red Fort.
- **Guided walking tours:** Several operators now offer guided heritage walks in Old Delhi, Mehrauli, and Nizamuddin. These can be booked online and are highly recommended for first-time visitors seeking deeper historical context.
- **Heritage e-rickshaws:** Many heritage areas now have dedicated electric rickshaws for eco-friendly last-mile connectivity from metro stations.

FIGURE: HOHO DELHI Sightseeing Bus. Contact.surojit, CC BY-SA 3.0 <https://creativecommons.org/licenses/by-sa/3.0>, via Wikimedia Commons

2.3 Google Maps and Apple maps

Having and using a decent maps application on one's phone is valuable in a place like Delhi, where often the roads are narrow and confusing, and it is easy to get lost. Even asking people for directions may help sometimes but not always!

Hence it is useful to install google maps (or Apple maps if one has an iPhone) and ideally download the maps of Delhi for offline use.

2.4 General Visitor Tips

- **Water:** Carry at least one litre of drinking water per person, especially from October to June. Bottled water is available near most monuments.
- **Dress:** Modest dress is advisable when visiting mosques, dargahs, and Sikh gurudwaras. Many require shoes to be removed and headscarves for women.
- **Timings:** Most ASI monuments open from sunrise to sunset (typically 7 AM to 6 PM in winter, 6 AM to 7 PM in summer). Some are closed on specific days — check the ASI website before visiting.
- **Guides:** Licensed guides can be hired at the entrance to major monuments such as the Red Fort, Qutub Minar, and Humayun's Tomb. Ensure they display their official badge from the Ministry of Tourism.
- **Photography:** Photography is permitted at most monuments. Video cameras and tripods may require special permits at some sites.

- **Respect:** Many of Delhi's monuments are active places of worship. Maintain silence and decorum inside mosques, dargahs, temples, and gurudwaras.

2.5 Conclusion

In this chapter we have discussed some of the resources to enable one to explore the various historical cities of Delhi.

Chapter 3: Qila Rai Pithora historical city of Delhi

In this chapter, we introduce Qila Rai Pithora, the first city of Delhi.

Figure: Depiction of Rajput king Prithviraj Chohan next to Qila Rai Pithora in Delhi, AI art generated by Dall E.

3.1 History of Qila Rai Pithora

This fort city named Qila Rai Pithora or Lal Kot was built during the reign of the Tomar Rajput king Anangpal Tomar and its construction was completed around 1060 AD. Anangpal is credited with the establishment of Delhi within its present-day boundaries, populating it and giving it the name Dhillika, later shortened to Dilli or Delhi. There is an iron pillar, currently part of the Qutub Minar complex, that has an inscription that records the founding of Dhillika by Anangpal in 1052 AD. Anangpal also established the Anangtal Baoli which is the oldest step well in Delhi.

The Chauhan king Vigraharaja captured Delhi from the Tomars in 12th century. His grandson was named Prithviraj Chauhan, who was the last of the kings from the Chauhan dynasty. Prithviraj ruled from Ajmer from 1177 to 1192 AD, and his reign also included Delhi. Finally, after losing the second battle of terrain in 1192 to Mohammed Ghori, an invader from the Ghurid dynasty in Afghanistan, his reign ended.

The Qila Rai Pithora fort walls extend in the current day areas of Saket, Mehrauli, and Sanjay Van areas. It was also called Lal Kot, although some historians have suggested that Lal Kot stands for the older and smaller fort and Qila Rai Pithora to the extended city that expanded later.

After defeating Prithviraj in battle, Mohammed Ghori made Delhi his capital and his slave general Qutubuddin Aibak started what is known as the slave dynasty. We cover the monuments in Mehrauli in the following chapter.

Figure: Depiction of life in Qila Rai Pithora

Figure: Gateway of the Qila Rai Pithora or Lal Kot fort. Mychel21, CC BY-SA 3.0 <https://creativecommons.org/licenses/by-sa/3.0>, via Wikimedia Commons

3.2 How to get to Qila Rai Pithora

For viewing some of the remaining extant walls of the Qila Rai Pithora fort, the nearest metro station is Saket. Google maps location: Qila Rai Pithora fort, Qila Lal Kot.

There is not actually much to see in Qila Rai Pithora, except a park and some fortifications, and a statue of Prithviraj Chauhan. A forest called Sanjay Van is next to the fort, so is Mehrauli archeological park. Parts of the walls of Qila Rai Pithora can be seen in these areas as well.

Figure: Remains of the fortifications of Qila Rai Pithora fort near Saket

Figure: Round bastions of Qila Rai Pithora or Lal Kot fort. Roboture, CC BY-SA 3.0 <https://creativecommons.org/licenses/by-sa/3.0>, via Wikimedia Commons

FIGURE: ARCHEOLOGICAL Survey of India notice for Qila Rai Pithora

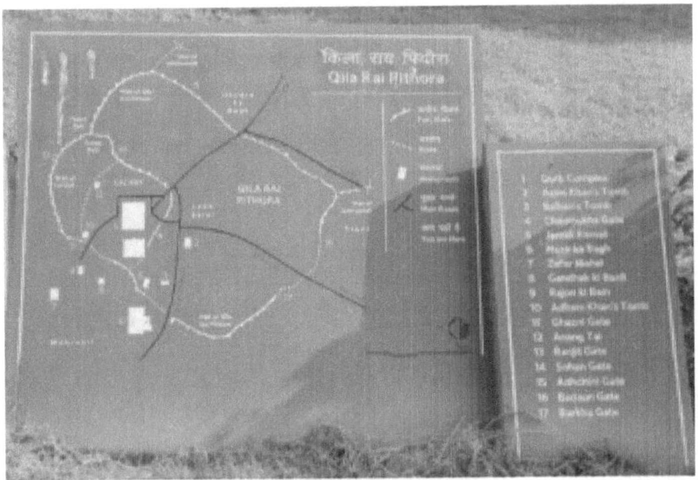

Figure: Plan of Qila Rai Pithora

Figure: Ancient Lal Kot Wall in Sanjay Van forest

3.3 Walk in Qila Rai Pithora

For the walk, take a metro to Saket station and then follow Google maps to the locations of Qila Rai Pithora, Prithviraj Chauhan Statue Delhi, Lal Kot Qila (within the Sanjay Van Forest). Follow the walls of the fort and try to imagine how it must have looked like in its prime.

3.4 Conclusion

In this chapter we have discussed about the first city of Delhi, Qila Rai Pithora, established by the Tomar king Anangpal Tomar, which is timed in the 11th century AD.

Chapter 4: Mehrauli historical city of Delhi

In this chapter, we introduce Mehrauli, a historical city of Delhi founded after the defeat of Prithviraj Chauhan by Mohammed Ghori in the second battle of Terain in 1192, thus heralding the Islamic conquest of India. Subsequently, Ghori's general Qutubuddin Aibak established the slave dynasty with Delhi as their new capital. Mehrauli is located near the area of Qila Rai Pithora, which was the earlier fort built by the Tomar and Chauhan kings of Delhi.

4.1 How to get to Mehrauli

Nearest metro station: Qutub Minar. From the metro station, the Qutub Minar is 1.5 km. Shared autos are available from the metro station to the Qutub Minar complex. One must buy tickets from the Archeological Survey of India tickets stand nearby the entrance. Distance from Qutub Minar Metro station to the entrance to Mehrauli archeological park and Jamali Kamali mosque is 1 km. Entrance to the archeological park is free, while Qutub complex entry needs a ticket.

Figure: Depiction of Qutub Minar in medieval times. AI art generated by Dall-E.

4.2 Things to see in Mehrauli

Mehrauli includes the Qutub Minar Complex, which includes the Qutub group of monuments such as Alai Minar, Iltutmish's tomb and a madrasa, and is a UNESCO world Heritage site.

Mehrauli also has Mehrauli archeological park, adjacent to the Qutub group of monuments, which contains historical monuments such as Jamali Kamali mosque, Balban's tomb, baoli, and others.

Mehrauli residential locality also has other historical monuments such as Zafar Mahal, palace of Bahadur Shah Zafar, the last Mughal emperor of Delhi.

4.3 Mehrauli archeological park

The Mehrauli archeological park lies between the Qutub Minar metro station and the Qutub Minar group of monuments. The signs of its exact location when viewed from the main road may not be very clear, so it is better to ask nearby people or use google maps.

Figure: Jamali Kamali Mosque in Mehrauli Archeological Park

The Mehrauli archeological park is spread over a wide area. One of the main buildings in the park is Jamali Kamali mosque and tomb, named after a Sufi saint and poet also called Shaikh Fazlullah or Jalal Khan, who lived during the Lodhi and early Mughal dynasty, and his follower. The mosque and tomb have beautiful architecture on the inside as well as on the exterior.

Figure: Rajon ki Baoli, or water well of kings, located in Mehrauli Archeological Park

Another of the important structures in Mehrauli archeological park is the Rajon ki baoli or water well of kings. There is another water well called Gandhak ki baoli also located in Mehrauli. These baolis were used for the water supply to the residents. Rajon ki baoli has some medieval structures built around it as well, which can be of interest.

Figure: Ruins of Balban's tomb in Mehrauli archeological park

Mehrauli archeological park also contains Balban's tomb, which belongs to Ghiyasuddin Balban, one of the sultans who succeeded Qutubuddin Aibak as sultan of Delhi. However, it is not very well maintained and probably is in need of repairs.

4.4 Qutub Minar Group of Monuments

The Qutub Minar group of monuments is just adjacent, even continuous with the Mehrauli archeological park, but its boundaries were demarcated probably as per the UNESCO world heritage site guidelines. One needs to buy a ticket from the ASI ticket booth to see these monuments.

These monuments were mainly constructed during or right after the reign of Qutubuddin Aibak, the first of the slave dynasty sultans and successor of Mohammed Ghori after his conquest of Delhi. Most of these buildings date from early or mid 13th century AD.

4.5 Qutub Minar

Figure: Qutub Minar in Mehrauli. Part of the World Heritage site Qutub Group of Monuments

Figure: Base of the Qutub Minar in Mehrauli. Part of the World Heritage site Qutub Group of Monuments

The most famous of the Qutub group is known as Qutub Minar or victory tower. Qutub Minar in Delhi is modelled after the minaret of Jam in Afghanistan (in the region where Ghori used to rule), but is much bigger in size. The walls are inscribed with Quranic verses. Its construction was started in 1193 by Qutubuddin Aibak soon after the defeat of Prithviraj Chauhan.

Qutub Minar is 72.5 metres tall — the world's tallest brick minaret.

Currently it is not allowed to climb the Qutub minar due to safety considerations. The minar was expanded by successive rulers after Qutubuddin, with each ruler adding a new storey at the top.

Figure: Iron Pillar in Mehrauli. Part of the World Heritage site Qutub Group of Monuments

4.6 Quwwat ul Islam Mosque and Iron Pillar

Quwwat ul Islam Mosque was the first mosque established in Delhi. It is in the form of a wide-open courtyard next to the Qutub Minar. Its pillars and bricks were taken from nearby Jain and Hindu temples which were demolished when the mosque was built, and whose architecture is clearly visible in the pillars of the mosque.

It also contains the iron pillar which was originally installed in Lal Kot by Anangpal Tomar, the first ruler of Delhi. The Iron Pillar is approximately 1,600 years old and has not rusted despite being outdoors for centuries — a remarkable metallurgical feat that continues to interest scientists today.

The new Islamic rulers of Delhi did not bring any architects with them from Afghanistan and so had to use the native Indian architects, as well as reuse materials from existing buildings such as temples. Hence it is a curious mix of Hindu, Jain and Muslim architecture.

Figure: Quwwat ul Islam Mosque, with ruins of temples used to build the pillars, in Mehrauli. Part of the World Heritage site Qutub Group of Monuments

4.7 Other monuments in the Qutub group

The other monuments in the Qutub group include the following

- Richly carved Alai Darwaza, just next to the Qutub minar.
- Tomb of Illutmish, who was the successor sultan to Qutubuddin Aibak. This also has richly carved walls with

verses from the Quran.

- Alai Minar. This was started by a later Sultan Alauddin Khalji in 1311. It was originally planned to be bigger than Qutub Minar but left incomplete due to various reasons.

FIGURE: ALAI DARWAZA in Mehrauli. Richly carved with verses from the Quran. Part of the World Heritage site Qutub Group of Monuments

Figure: Tomb of Iltutmish in Mehrauli. Walls are richly carved with verses from the Quran. Part of the World Heritage site Qutub Group of Monuments

Figure: Madrasa next to Qutub Minar in Mehrauli. Part of the World Heritage site Qutub Group of Monuments

Figure: Alai Minar in Mehrauli. Part of the World Heritage site Qutub Group of Monuments

4.8 Other monuments in Mehrauli area

Mehrauli was a thriving residential area in medieval times. Aside from the Qutub complex and archeological park, a number of other historical monuments are present here as well, in the middle of the residential area. These include some Mughal era monuments as well.

Figure: Adam Khan Tomb in Mehrauli near Mehrauli bus station

Adham Khan's tomb, also called Bhul Bhulaiya or labyrinth, is the tomb of one of the generals of Mughal emperor Akbar. It was built in 1562 and is protected by the Archeological survey of India. It is located opposite the Mehrauli bus station.

Figure: Zafar Mahal in Mehrauli. Named after the last Mughal emperor Bahadur Shah Zafar

Another important monument in Mehrauli is Zafar Mahal, named after Bahadur Shah Zafar who was the last Mughal emperor till he was deposed by the British in 1857. The main building of Zafar Mahal was constructed in 1842 by Akbar Shah II, one of the earlier Mughal emperors, and its entrance gate was constructed by Bahadur Shah Zafar. It has a lot of historical importance, but unfortunately it stands neglected today.

Figure: Mahavir statue at the Jain temple Ahimsa Sthal in Mehrauli

The Mehrauli area also contains a few Jain temples and ashrams. It is to be noted that the pillars of Quwwat ul Islam Mosque in Qutub group of monuments were built by the ruins of the some of the existing Jain temples, indicating their presence before the conquest by Ghori. One such Jain temple is Ahmisa Sthal, which is located on a small hillock directly opposite Mehrauli archeological park and a short walking distance from the Qutub group of monuments (between the Qutub minar and metro station). It is a peaceful place to visit and meditate.

4.9 Walk in Mehrauli

Take the metro to Qutub Minar Metro station, from there walk to the Mehrauli archeological park and see the Jamali Kamali mosque, baoli, Balban's tomb, Metcalf canopy. Then cross the road and view the

Ahimsa Sthal Jain temple. Finally walk to Qutub Minar complex, buy the ticket from the ASI stall and view the Qutub group of monuments.

4.10 Conclusion

In this chapter, we have discussed the historical monuments of Mehrauli area.

Chapter 5: Siri historical city of Delhi

In this chapter, we discuss about Siri, another of the historical cities of Delhi.

Siri mainly encompasses the areas around Siri fort as well as the present day Hauz Khas. The fortifications of Siri were built by the Khalji kings of Delhi, particularly Alauddin Khalji, as a way to protect the city from repeated and frequent Mongol invasions. The Siri fort was completed around 1307 AD. Hauz Khas tank was constructed by Alauddin Khalji to provide water to the Siri fort residents, and later expanded with a madrasa and other constructions by the Tughlaq rulers who followed the Khalji rulers.

Figure: Depiction of Alauddin Khilji. AI art generated by Dall-e

5.1 How to get to Siri fort and Hauz Khas

For getting to Siri fort, one needs to visit the area named as Shahpur Jat, around which some of the fortifications are visible. There is a Sports

Complex and an auditorium, both with the same name Siri Fort and located close to the same area. Siri Fort is around 1.5 km distance from Hauz Khas metro station, and it is close to the Asian games village near Shahpur Jat.

For getting to Hauz Khas complex and Madrasa and tank, the nearest Metro Station is Hauz Khas. From the metro station, one can either walk to Hauz Khas village (2.1 km) or preferably take an auto rickshaw. From Hauz Khas village to the fort complex is around 400 m walking. Google maps location is Hauz Khas Fort. One needs to buy tickets for entry to the fort, which can be paid either in cash, or online by scanning the QR code at the entrance.

Figure: Depiction of a procession of war elephants in Siri

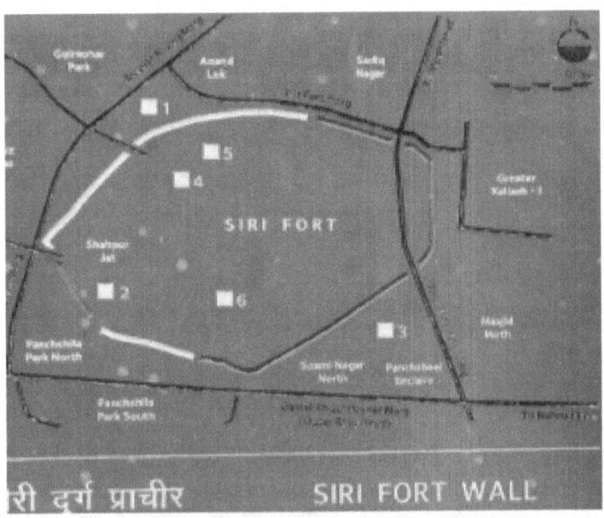

Figure: Plan of the Siri Fort

Figure: Walls of the historic Siri fort and Tohfe Wala Gumbad. Varun Shiv Kapur, CC BY 2.0 <https://creativecommons.org/licenses/by/2.0>, via Wikimedia Commons

5.2 Siri Fort

Siri fort was built by Sultan Alauddin Khalji by employing 70000 workers, it is said. It is in an oval shape and originally had seven gates, out of which only one of the gates, the south-eastern gate, is still surviving. The walls were massive in size and thickness to deter the mongol invaders.

Figure: Mohammad wali masjid. Siri fort area

Mohammad wali masjid is a beautiful mosque located inside the siri fort area. It is enclosed by a wall and a gate and a garden around it.

Figure: Tohfe wala Gumbad. Siri Fort area

Tohfe wala gumbad is another of the structures inside the Siri fort walls. Its name means that it was gifted, but who made the gift and to whom is not known. It is actually a mosque, built with simple architecture.

5.3 Hauz Khas tank and fort complex

Haus Khas is the name of the royal tank or lake. It was built by Sultan Alauddin Khalji of the Khalji dynasty and completed around 1354 AD. There is a madrasa (Islamic seminary) and other buildings next to the royal tank, which were added by the Khalji rulers and later Tughlaq rulers including Firoz Shah Tughlaq. The purpose of the lake or royal tank was to provide water to the residents of the Siri fort.

To get to the Hauz Khas tank, one needs to take the metro to Hauz Khas and get an autorickshaw from there to Haus Khas village entrance. From there walk to the madrasa and fort and Haus Khas tank.

Note than the entrance to the Hauz Khas tank area is via the deer park, which is different from the entrance to the madrasa and fort which is through Hauz Khas village. Also, a ticket is needed for the Hauz Khas fort and madrasa, while the deer park and tank are free to view.

Figure: Domed buildings at the northern wing of Hauz Khas Madrasa

Figure: Tughlaq era tombs in Hauz Khas complex

The Hauz Khas fort complex, which is ticketed and managed by Archeological Survey of India, consists of a number of buildings including multiple Tughlaq era tombs, domed pavilions, gardens, a madrasa and a mosque.

The Hauz Khas madrasa, or Islamic seminary, was built in 1352 under Sultan Firoz Shah. It was one of the famous madrasas under the Delhi sultanate, and lots of students came to study and train in Islamic theology. The madrasa is built on multiple floors and its architecture, with windows, pillars and chattris, and overlooking the Hauz Khas lake, is amazing to observe.

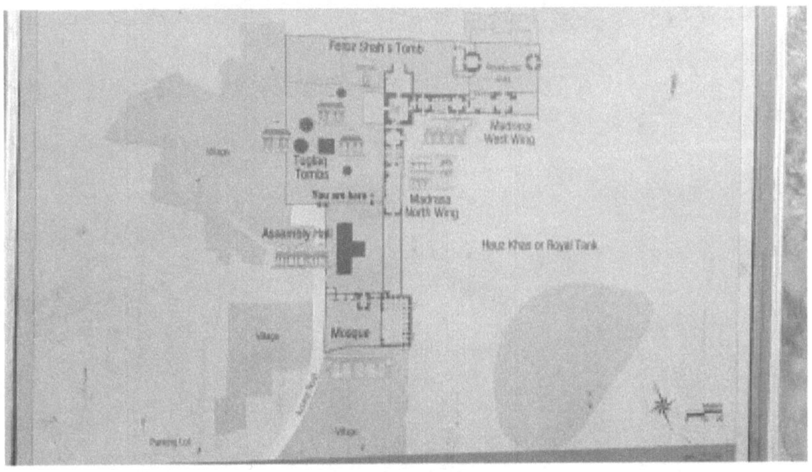

Figure: Site plan of the Hauz Khas Complex

Figure: Madrasa building at Hauz Khas complex, viewed from the lake level

Figure: Feroze Shah Tomb in Hauz Khas Complex

Sultan Feroze Shah Tughlaq's tomb and the other tombs in the Hauz Khas complex are also interesting. Notice the roof and the decorations on the walls. The domed buildings at the northern end of the madrasa are also a sight to watch.

Figure: Hauz Khas lake or royal tank

The Hauz Khas tank, coming from the deer park near the tank, is a relaxing place to enjoy. It is spread over quite a large area, with an island at the center of the tank. One can also enjoy viewing the variety of animals at the deer park next to the tank.

5.4 Walks in Siri

For a walk in Siri fort, take an autorickshaw from Hauz Khas metro station to the Siri fort near Asian Games village. From there take a walk and explore the remains of the Siri fort and the other structures including Mohammad wali masjid and Tohfe Wala Gumbad.

For a walk in the Hauz Khas complex, take the metro to Hauz Khas metro station and an autorickshaw to Hauz Khas village entrance. The fort complex is located at the end of the upscale village, about half a km walk. The village has lots of trendy shops and cafes and art galleries. Buy the ticket at the ASI booth and view the Hauz Khas complex. Then go back to the Hauz Khas village entrance and to the deer park, from there view the deer and other animals and finally walk to Hauz Khas tank.

5.5 Conclusion

In this chapter we have discussed about the historical city of Siri and the various buildings and the tank that are part of it.

Chapter 6: Jahanpanah and Tughlaqabad, historical cities of Delhi

In this chapter we explore Jahanpanah and Tughlaqabad, which are part of the historical cities of Delhi. These were both established by the Tughlaq rulers of Delhi. Today, Tughlaqabad mainly includes the Tughlaqabad fort, Adilabad fort and Ghiyasuddin Tughlaq's tomb. Jahanpanah (meaning refuge of the world) includes some structures such as Bijay Mandal and Begumpuri mosque.

Figure: Depiction of the people of Delhi migrating to Dhaulagiri or Daulatabad under the orders of Mohammed Bin Tughlaq. But eventually they had to return to Delhi. AI art generated by Dall-e

6.1 How to get there

The nearest metro station to Tughlaqabad fort is Tughlaqabad (4.4 km distance). One needs to take an auto rickshaw to the fort since the distance is not easily walkable. The Google maps location is

Tughlaqabad Fort. For visiting the fort, one needs to buy a ticket from the Archeological Survey of India ticket counter. Ghiyasuddin Tughlaq's tomb is across the main road from the entrance of Tughlaqabad fort, and its entrance is part of the same ticket. However, one needs to buy the ticket first near the Tughlaqabad fort entrance before visiting the tomb across the road.

Warning: There are many monkeys at or around the Tughlaqabad Fort, who may try to snatch eatables from visitors to the fort and tomb.

For getting to Bijay Mandal and Begumpuri mosque, which are located in present day Kalu Sarai and Malviya Nagar within the limits of Jahanpanah, the nearest metro station is Hauz Khas. Bijay Mandal and Begumpuri mosque are both within walking distance (within 600m) from the Hauz Khas metro station.

Figure: Depiction of life in Jahanpanah

6.2 Introduction to Tughlaqabad Fort

Tughlaqabad Fort was built by Ghiyasuddin Tughlaq, the capable leader and noblemen of the Khalji court who established the Tughlaq Dynasty after the Khaljis and became Sultan of Delhi, in 1321. Ghiyasuddin is credited with defeating and foiling the plans of the mongol invaders multiple times, and the size of the massive walls of the Tughlaqabad fort testifies to this.

Unfortunately, the fort was abandoned in 1327, two years after Ghiyasuddin's sudden death in 1325 and never saw a long-term resident population inside the fort. After his death, either because of accident or conspiracy, his son and successor Mohammed Bin Tughlaq became the sultan and soon decided to shift his capital to Deogiri or Daulatabad in central India.

Figure: Depiction of soldiers guarding the fortress of Tughlaqabad

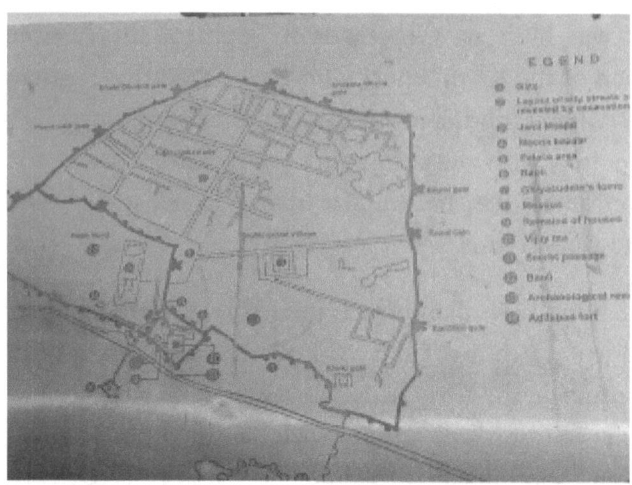

Figure: Layout of the Tughlaqabad Fort and surroundings

Figure: Massive walls of Tughlaqabad fort

6.3 Structures in Tughlaqabad Fort

Tughlaqabad Fort today is mostly in ruins, but the parts that are still standing, especially the massive outer stone walls of the fort, make an impressive sight.

There are multiple buildings in various states of ruin, including ruins of the palace and watch towers. There is also an inner citadel that one can climb on the top and enjoy a good view of the surroundings. There is also a basement structure inside the fort called Meena bazaar that used to be a flourishing market. Much of the fort has been long since taken over by residential colonies.

Figure: View of Ghiyasuddin Tughlaq's tomb from Tughlaqabad Fort

Figure: View of nearby housing settlements from the top of Tughlaqabad Fort

Figure: View of the fortifications from the top of Tughlaqabad Fort

Figure: Ghiyasuddin Tughlaq's tomb

6.4 Ghiyasuddin Tughlaq's tomb and mausoleum

To get to Ghiyasuddin's tomb, one needs to exit the Tughlaqabad fort completely, go to the main Mehrauli Badarpur road and cross it. The tomb is directly opposite the fort and is in fact viewable from the top of the fort. It too has been protected by high walls and is reached via an elevated path or causeway leading to a gateway built of red sandstone.

The tomb itself is massive, consisting of a single white marble dome with sloping walls. The external is built of red sandstone. Inside the mausoleum are three graves, that of the Sultan Ghiyasuddin Tughlaq, his wife and his son and successor Mohammed Bin Tughlaq. There is also a nearby tomb in the same complex but outside the actual mausoleum, that of Zafar Khan, a famous general of the Delhi sultans.

Figure: Exterior of Adilabad Fort. Ramesh lalwani, CC BY-SA 4.0 <https://creativecommons.org/licenses/by-sa/4.0>, via Wikimedia Commons

6.5 Adilabad Fort

Adilabad Fort is located close to Tughlaqabad fort. It was an earlier structure, built in the 14th century, before the Tughlaq dynasty but was repaired and expanded by Mohammed Bin Tughlaq.

Figure: Ruins of Bijay mandal palace. Varun Shiv Kapur, CC BY 2.0 <https://creativecommons.org/licenses/by/2.0>, via Wikimedia Commons

6.6 Historical structures in Jahanpanah

Jahanpanah was the city built and promoted by Mohammed Bin Tughlaq, the son of Ghiyasuddin. Today its remains consists of a number of buildings scattered around South Delhi, especially around Malviya Nagar, Panchsheel Enclave and Greater Kailash.

One of the main structures is the Bijay Mandal·palace complex, situated around Malviya Nagar and walking distance from Hauz Khas metro station.

Bijay Mandal and surrounding monuments were built during the reign of Mohammed Bin Tughlaq, to serve as the royal residence. Sadly most of these buildings are in a state of ruin.

Figure: Entry gate for Begumpuri mosque. Varun Shiv Kapur, CC BY 2.0 <https://creativecommons.org/licenses/by/2.0>, via Wikimedia Commons

Another of the structures is Begumpuri mosque, situated near the Bijay Mandal and walking distance from Aurobindo Ashram, in Begumpur village. It has only one dome.

There are other scattered structures in Jahanpanah around upscale localities in South Delhi such as Greater Kailash and Malviya Nagar. Examples include Lal Gumbad, tomb of a Sufi saint. Another interesting structure is Kharbuze ka Gumbad, which resembles a sliced musk melon in shape, and is located within the precincts of a school.

6.7 Walk in Tughlaqabad and Jahanpanah

For the walk in Tughlaqabad, take the metro to Tughlaqabad station and from there take an autorickshaw to Tughlaqabad fort for 4.5 km. Then buy the tickets and spend some time exploring the different parts of the fort. Climb to the top pavilion and view the surrounding areas as well. Finally exit the Tughlaqabad fort, cross the Mehrauli Badarpur road and walk to Ghiyasuddin Tughlaq's tomb. Notice the exterior of the tomb and its sloping walls and beautiful white marble dome. Also note the graves and architecture inside. Adilabad fort is also walking distance from Tughlaqabad.

For viewing the structures in Jahanpanah, take the metro to Hauz Khas metro station, exit from the Panchasheel enclave side and walk from there. The google maps locations are Begumpuri mosque and Bijay Mandal.

6.8 Conclusion

In this chapter we discussed about the Tughlaqabad fort and tomb, which form the main surviving structures of the historical city of Jahapanah, which flourished during the Tughlaq dynasty rule of Delhi.

Chapter 7: Ferozabad historical city of Delhi

In this chapter we discuss Ferozabad, the historical city of Delhi established by Feroze Shah Tughlaq.

7.1 How to get there

The nearest metro stations to Feroze Shah Kotla fort are ITO (700 m distance) and Delhi gate (1 km). One can either walk or take an auto rickshaw from the metro station. Google maps location is Feroz Shah Kotla Fort. There are a number of green parks adjoining the fort. A famous cricket stadium, established in 1883, that used to be called Feroze Shah Kotla Stadium and now changed to Arun Jaitley Stadium, is established nearby.

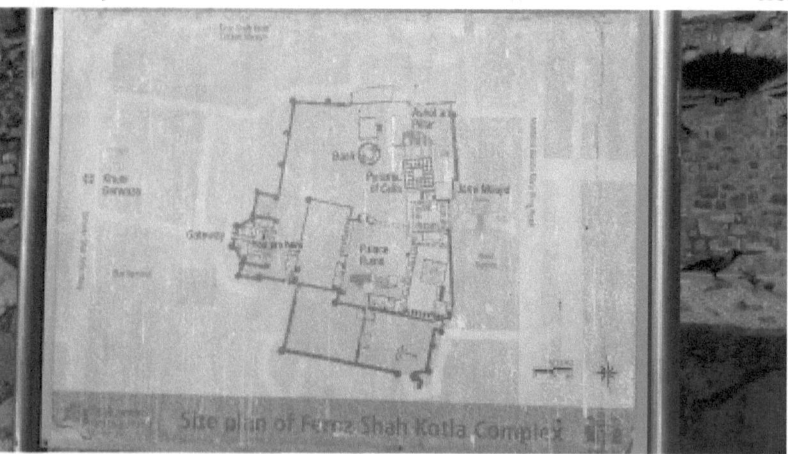

Figure: Site plan of Feroze Shah Kotla complex

Figure: Depiction of life in Ferozabad

7.2 Introduction to Ferozabad and Feroze Shah Kotla Fort

Feroze Shah Kotla fort was established by Sultan Feroze Shah Tughlaq in 1354 AD as the main site of his new capital city of Ferozabad. Feroz Shah Tughlaq's reign in Delhi was comparatively long lasting, from 1351 to 1388. He was a relatively benevolent sultan, focusing on much-needed political stability, patronage of the ulema and the welfare of his subjects. He was also big on architecture and improving the infrastructure of his kingdom, establishing a number of rest houses, sarais, reservoirs and tombs. He got an Ashoka pillar brought respectfully from Topra Kalan in Haryana and established it in his capital at Feroze Shah Kotla fort. However, his lenience as a ruler also led to a number of rebellions and weakened the kingdom in the long run.

Figure: The fort entrance with arched gateways at Feroze Shah Kotla

Figure: Palace ruins in the fort at Feroze Shah Kotla

7.3 Structures at Feroze Shah Kotla fort

The fort entrance is ticketed, so one needs to buy a ticket at the ASI ticket office, or online.

Figure: The Ashoka Pillar on top of the pyramidal structure at Feroze Shah Kotla fort

Figure: Inscriptions on the Ashoka Pillar at Feroze Shah Kotla

Figure: Baoli or water well at Feroze Shah Kotla

Figure: The mosque at Feroze Shah Kotla

The main structures at Feroze Shah Kotla include

- Wall and arched gateways
- A multi- floor pyramidal structure that contains the Ashoka pillar
- Jami masjid or congregational mosque
- Ruins of the royal palace consisting of the Diwan e Khas and

Diwan-e-aam

- A baoli or water well inside the fort premises

Note: Feroze Shah Kotla Fort is also famous locally for its association with djinn (spirits) according to popular folklore. Every Thursday, many Delhiites visit to leave offerings and petitions in crevices of the walls, a folk tradition that has continued for generations and was memorably described by William Dalrymple in City of Djinns.

7.4 Walk at Feroze Shah Kotla

For walking through the fort, take the metro to ITO or Delhi Gate and walk from there to the location of the Feroze Shah Kotla fort. Buy the tickets from the ASI stand and enter the fort. Observe the walls and the arched gateways, the palace ruins and the pyramidal structure with Ashoka pillar on top. Ascend the steps to the mosque and also view the baoli or water well. Have a look at the surrounding structures as well.

7.5 Conclusion

In this chapter we have discussed the historical city of Ferozabad, which mainly consists of the Feroze Shah Kotla fort and surroundings.

Chapter 8: Sher Garh historical city of Delhi

In this chapter, we discuss yet another historical city of Delhi, that of Sher Garh. This city was established in the 16th century and is located around central Delhi. It consists of Purana Qila fort and the area of Humayun's tomb and Nizamuddin Auliya's dargah.

Sher Garh is the city founded by Sher Shah Suri in 1550s and mainly includes the Purana Qila and surrounding areas. It also includes the incomplete city of Dinpanah that was started by Humayun and built over by Sher Shah after defeating Humayun in battle. The Lodi Gardens (although it was built at the time of the Lodi sultans), Purana Qila, Humayun's tomb and Nizamuddin area, including the Sunder Nursery archeological area and garden would be included in this area.

Figure: Depiction of Sher Shah Suri in Purana Qila. AI generated art by Dall-e

8.1 How to get there

For Purana Qila fort, the nearest metro stations are Pragati Maidan (2.1 km distance) and Khan market (2.9 km). One can take an auto rickshaw from the metro station or walk the distance. Google maps location is Purana Qila. Purana Qila fort is located next to Delhi Zoo.

For Humayun's tomb and Nizamuddin, the nearest metro station is Jangpura (0.7 km) from where one can walk or take a rickshaw or auto rickshaw or sometimes a shared rickshaw. For Humayun's tomb, one needs to purchase an ASI ticket. For Sunder Nursery there is a separate ticket that needs to be purchased. For Lodi Gardens the nearest metro station is Jor Bagh (850 m).

Figure: Depiction of life in Dinpanah / Sher Garh

8.2 Introduction to Sher Garh and Purana Qila

The construction of the fort of Purana Qila or Kila-e-Kohna started around 1530 AD. It was built partly by the Mughal emperor Humayun and partly by Sher Shah Suri who had defeated him. Humayun's city was named by him as Dinpanah and was constructed between 1530 and 1538. Sher Shah Suri succeeded him in 1540, strengthened its walls and started making additions to the earlier Humayun's fort. It then became known as Sher Garh after Sher Shah Suri's name. Hem Chandra Vikramaditya, the successor of Sher Shah Suri, was crowned at Sher Garh, before losing to Akbar in the second battle of Panipat at 1556.

However, the site holds much older constructions that were excavated by the Archeological Survey of India, which unearthed traces of an Iron age culture that had painted grey ware. Some believe that it was the area of Indraprastha, the kingdom of the Pandavas described in the epic Mahabharata and also mentioned in Buddhist literature of the Mauryan period as Indapatta or Indapattana, the capital of the Kuru kingdom on the banks of the Yamuna River. In fact, a village named Inderpat existed later at that very site, whose name was also inspired by the Pandava kingdom.

Figure: The Bada Darwaza, main entrance gate for Purana Qila.

Figure: Site plan of Purana Qila

8.3 Purana Qila

One needs to buy a ticket from the ASI ticket counter to enter Purana Qila fort. It is located close to the entrance of Delhi Zoo.

Figure: Archeological Museum in Purana Qila. Near the entrance

The fortress of Purana Qila includes a number of buildings. The archeological museum is just next to the main entrance besides the majestic fort walls. The museum holds specimens of archaeological findings excavated from Purana Qila and nearby sites.

Figure: Humayun Gate or Humayun Darwaza at Purana Qila

Figure: Talaaqi Darwaza gate of Purana Qila

Purana Qila has a number of majestic gates or Darwazas. These include the Bara Darwaza or Big Gate that faces west, the Humayun Darwaza that faces south towards the Humayun's tomb, and the Talaqi gate or forbidden gate.

Figure: Excavations at Purana Qila

Figure: Excavations at Purana Qila

As mentioned earlier, Purana Qila is rich in history for thousands of years and has been the site of archeological excavations by the archeological survey of India. Some of the excavations are still ongoing.

Figure: Qila e Quhna Masjid in Purana Qila: Exterior View

Figure: Qila e Quhna Masjid in Purana Qila: Interior View

One of the important buildings inside the Purana Qila fort is the Qila e Quhna mosque. It was built by Sher Shah Suri in 1541 and consists of a single dome, and is a good example of pre Mughal mosque architecture. It has got ornate Jharokhas built in Rajasthani style on the first floor, which can be viewed from the front as well as behind the mosque. It is rich in calligraphy with verses from the Quran inscribed on the walls.

Figure: Sher Mandal structure at Purana Qila

Another important structure in Purana Qila fort is an octagonal two floored structure called Sher Mandal, also built by Sher Shah Suri in 1540s. It is built in a mixture of Timurid and Savafid style of architecture. After conquering the Purana Qila fort and defeating the successors of Sher Shah Suri, the Mughal emperor Humayun used this Sher Mandal building as a library. It was from the steps of this very building that Humayun fell in an accident to his death in 1556.

Figure: Baoli at Purana Qila

The Baoli or water well is another important structure in Purana Qila. Its function was to store and provide water to the inhabitants.

Figure: Humayun's tomb from ground level. Part of Humayun's tomb complex

Figure: Humayun's tomb from first floor level. Part of Humayun's tomb complex

8.3 Humayun's Tomb Complex

Humayun's Tomb Complex is located to the south of Purana Qila. It is a UNESCO World Heritage site and said to be one of the inspirations for the Taj Mahal. One needs to buy the tickets at the entrance from the ASI ticket booth.

Humayun's tomb was built by Humayun's widow, Hamida Banu Begam, after his death. It is a good example of Mughal gardens and Mughal architecture in general. It has the tomb not only of Humayun but also his wives Bega Begum, Hamida Begum, Mughal prince Dara Shikoh, and later Mughal emperors including Farrukh Siyar. It has historical significance as well, being the site from where the last Mughal emperor Bahadur Shah Zafar was captured by the British after the 1857 war.

Figure: View of the surrounding Mughal Gardens from Humayun's tomb. Part of Humayun's tomb complex

Humayun's tomb is built out of red sandstone, combined with white marble at places. The symmetry of the structure when seen from various angles is amazing. It is modelled as a garden of paradise as mentioned in the Quran and many examples of which are available in Iran. It is inspired by Persian architecture. The windows in the main tomb building are covered with intricate jaalis or perforated latticed screens made of stone.

Figure: View inside Humayun's tomb. Part of Humayun's tomb complex

Figure: Isa Khan's tomb, part of the Humayun's tomb complex

Other monuments that are part of the Humayun's tomb complex include the following:

- Tomb and mosque of Isa Khan, an Afghan noble and general in the court of Sher Shah Suri.
- Afsarwala tomb and mosque, which was named after a military commander
- Bu Halima's gateway and Garden
- Arab Sarai, which was a rest house for travelers

Figure: Sufi saint Sheikh Nizamuddin Auliya's dargah and mosque

8.4 Sheikh Nizamuddin Auliya's Dargah

Sheikh Nizamuddin Auliya was a famous Sufi saint of the Indian subcontinent, highly respected by the Delhi Sultans. He lived from 1238 to 1325 AD. His tomb in Nizamuddin area of Delhi, close to Humayun's tomb, is revered by both Hindus and Muslims today. There is always a crowd of worshippers at the dargah, and qawwali songs to Allah in the Sufi style are sung at the dargah during nighttime, especially on Thursday nights.

Figure: Tomb of Mirza Ghalib, close to dargah of Sufi Saint Sheikh Nizamuddin Auliya

Figure: Chausath Khamba or 64 pillars, next to Mirza Ghalib's tomb and close to dargah of Sufi Saint Sheikh Nizamuddin Auliya

Figure: Celebrated medieval poet Abdur Rahim Khan-e-Khanum's tomb

Many nobles of the Delhi court, poets and intellectuals, and even Sultans and Mughal emperors thought it auspicious to be buried close to the dargah of such a great saint as Sheikh Nizamuddin. Hence, there are a number of graves, tombs and mausoleums in the vicinity of Sheikh Nizamuddin's Dargah.

These include the graves and tombs of Amir Khusro, Abdul Rahim Khan-e-Khanum and Mirza Ghalib, all famous poets. Humayun's tomb itself is not too far from the dargah. Sunder nursery area also contains a number of such graves and tombs. So has Lodi gardens. Safdarjung's tomb is also close by.

Figure: Poster at entrance to Sunder nursery archeological park and garden

8.5 Sunder Nursery

Sunder nursery is an archeological park and garden. It covers the area between Humayun's tomb and Purana Qila fort.

The area includes some tombs including Mirza Muzaffar Husain's tomb, Sundar Wala Burj and Lakkarwala Burj. Many of the graves are richly decorated inside.

Figure: Interior of Sunder Wala Burj in Sunder Nursery. Richly decorated and carved with Quranic verses.

Figure: Exterior of Mirza Muzaffar Hussain's tomb in Sunder Nursery.

Figure: Interior of Mirza Muzaffar Hussain's tomb in Sunder Nursery.

8.6 Lodi Gardens

Lodi gardens are from the Lodi era, which were the dynasty of the Delhi sultanate just before the Mughal invader Babar defeated the last Lodi sultan Ibrahim Lodi in the first battle of Panipat in 1526.

Figure: Lodhi Era mosque (16th century) next to Bada Gumbad in Lodhi Gardens in Delhi

Figure: Richly carved Lodhi Era mosque (16th century) next to Bada Gumbad in Lodhi Gardens in Delhi

Figure: Sheesh Gumbad and Bada Gumbad in Lodhi gardens in Delhi

Figure: Fortifications around the tomb of Sikandar Lodhi. In Lodhi gardens in Delhi

The Lodi gardens include the following:

- Tomb of Sikandar Lodi, Lodi Sultan preceding Ibrahim Lodi, with walls surrounding it
- Shish Gumbad and the Bara Gumbad, two Lodi era tombs from the 15th – 16th century.
- A three domed mosque next to the Bada Gumbad
- Tomb of Mohammed Shah Sayyid, sultan of the Sayyid dynasty
- A lake and gardens with a variety of trees, birds and insects.

These are also located west of the Sundar nursery.

8.7 Walks in the area of Sher Garh

For a walk in Purana Qila, the nearest metro station is Pragati Maidan metro which is 2.1 km away. One can walk from there or take an auto and explore Purana Qila. There are a number of archeological sites close to Purana Qila across Mathura Road, such as Sher Shah Suri Gate and Khairul Manzil Mosque, which can be covered in the same walk.

To walks in the Humayun's tomb complex, the nearest metro stations include Jawaharlal Nehru Stadium (2 km), Hazrat Nizamuddin (3 km) from where one can take an autorickshaw or a cycle-rickshaw to the Humayun's tomb and buy the tickets. Sunder Nursery is just across the road from Humayun's tomb. So, both of them can be covered in the same walk.

To visit the Hazrat Nizamuddin Dargah, one can go to metro station called Hazrat Nizamuddin from where shared autos to the gali near the dargah are readily available. Alternatively, it is walking distance from the Humayun Tomb complex and Sunder Nursery and therefore can be also included in the same walk.

For a walk in the Lodi gardens, one can take the metro to Khan Market (1 km) or Jor Bagh (850 m) metro station, and walk from there.

8.8 Conclusion

In this chapter we have discussed the Sher Garh historical city located in central Delhi, which dates from the 16th century. This includes the Purana Qila fort and surrounding historical areas, including Hazrat Nizamuddin Dargah, Humayun's tomb, Sunder nursery and Lodi gardens.

Chapter 9: Shahjahanabad historical city of Delhi

In this chapter we discuss the historical city of Shahjahanabad, which was the capital of the Mughal empire from the time of Shah Jahan.

Shahjahanabad is the city that was established by the Mughal emperor Shah Jahan in 1638 AD after he shifted his capital to Delhi from Agra. It contains the Red fort, Jama Masjid and other buildings. It is often synonymous with the old city of Delhi, and also sometimes simply called "Old Delhi". Although its glory declined somewhat after the British took over, there is a lot of history still present in its walls, narrow lanes and bustling markets, which can be viewed by one and all.

Figure: Mughal emperor Shah Jahan giving audience at the Red Fort in Delhi. AI generated art by Dall-e

Shahjahanabad is a walled city, and some of the walls and gates to the old city are still standing, although most were demolished by the British after the 1857 war and mutiny. Examples of the remaining gates of Shahjahanabad include Kashmere gate and Ajmeri Gate and Mori Gate. It historical limits included localities such as Daryaganj, Paharganj, and Karolbagh. It includes bazars such as Chandni Chowk with narrow streets full of shops, havelis such as Mirza Ghalib's haveli, and religious buildings including temples, mosques, gurudwaras and churches. It is also a culinary treat, with a number of famous food and sweet shops.

Figure: Depiction of life in Shahjahanabad during Mughal times

9.1 How to reach Shahjahanabad

The nearest metro station is Red Fort and it is located directly opposite to the Red Fort complex, a UNESCO world heritage site. One needs to buy tickets from the ASI ticket counter at red fort, or pay online for tickets at the ASI website.

Across the road from Shahjahanabad is the historical Chandni Chowk market with its many narrow lanes or Galis such as Parathewali gali.

Figure: Front view of the Red fort. Part of the Red Fort Complex

Figure: Lahori Gate Entrance gate of the Red Fort. Part of the Red Fort Complex

9.2 The Red Fort Complex

The Red Fort Complex, also called Lal Qila, is a UNESCO world Heritage Site and contains the main palaces of the Mughal emperors of Delhi. One needs to buy a ticket from Archeological Survey of India (ASI) ticket office, to visit the Red Fort. It is made of Red Sandstone, similar to the Agra Fort, hence the name Red Fort.

The Red fort has a number of gates, the most famous of them being the Lahori Gate, from which the Prime Minister of India unfurls the Indian flag and gives a speech on 15th August Independence Day each year. There is a market named Chatta Chowk right after entering this gate, where a number of jewelry and handicrafts shops are available for visitors to buy souvenirs.

Figure: Chatta Chowk market at the Red Fort. Part of the Red Fort Complex

Figure: Diwan e Aam in the Red Fort. Where the Mughal emperor gave public audiences. Part of the Red Fort Complex

On entering the red fort one, can see the Diwan e Aam or Audience Hall, where the Mughal emperor used to give public audiences and hear requests and grievances from the public.

There are also a number of museums available on the Red Fort Complex, on the theme of India's independence, established in the barracks which formerly used to house the British army soldiers. These include the 1857 war museum, Indian independence museum, Jallianwala Bagh museum and Subhash Chandra Bose and INA museum. The tickets for the museums need to be purchased at the entrance to the Red Fort in advance.

Figure: Mughal buildings in the Red Fort. Part of the Red Fort Complex

Figure: Interior of Diwan e khas in the Red Fort. Part of the Red Fort Complex

Figure: Red fort barracks, now housing the museums

Further inside, there are a number of beautiful buildings including the following:

- Naubat Khana or drum house, which is at the entrance to the palace area
- Mumtaz Mahal or Women's quarters
- Rang Mahal or palace of color, part of the women's quarters for the harem
- Khas Mahal, the Mughal emperor's private residence
- Diwan e Khas or hall of private audience, where the emperor received state guests
- Hammam or imperial bath
- Moti Masjid, a mosque built out of marble.
- There was also a water supply from the river Yamuna through canals that were called Nahar e Bishist.

9.3 Salimgarh Fort

Salimgarh Fort is a part of the Red Fort complex but was an earlier construction than the Red Fort itself, being built in 1546 by Salim Shah, a successor of Sher Shah Suri. A red arched bridge called Bahadur Shah Gate links it to the Red Fort.

Salimgarh Fort used to function as a prison for the Mughals as well as the British. It is located at one end of the Red Fort complex and can be visited on the same ticket. One can view the prison cells where the freedom fighters against British rule were imprisoned.

Figure: Jama Masjid in Old Delhi, opposite Red Fort Complex. Built by Mughal Emperor Shah Jahan and one of the largest mosques in India

9.4 Jama Masjid

Jama Masjid, originally called Masjid-i-Jehan-Numa, is a huge mosque also built by emperor Shah Jahan and located across the road from the Red Fort. It is one of the largest mosques in India, and can house up to 25000 worshippers during the time of namaz.

The metro station Jama Masjid is closest to this.

Jama Masjid can be visited outside prayer times by non-muslims as well. One must take off their shoes and keep it with one of the many shoe keepers on the steps of the Jama Masjid. One can also climb the steps of the tower of the Jama masjid after paying a ticket fee, to get an amazing bird's eye view of Old Delhi.

9.5 Gates of Shahjahanabad

One can visit the few remaining gates of the walled city of Shajahanabad. For example, Kashmere gate or the northern gate is located near the Kashmere Gate ISBT bus station.

Figure: Kashmere Gate. One of the Mughal era gates of Shahjahanabad, old city of Delhi.

9.6 Chandni Chowk

Chandni Chowk is the most famous of the Mughal era markets of Delhi. It starts from the street directly across Red Fort and runs until Fatehpuri mosque. The name "Chandni Chowk" or Moonlight square was given since it had canals that reflected moonlight and shone in the night under the rays of the moon.

Chandni Chowk Redevelopment: In recent years, the Delhi government undertook a significant redevelopment of the Chandni Chowk streetscape, removing encroachments and creating a pedestrianised central promenade. This has made the main street considerably more walkable for visitors, though the galis remain characteristically busy.

The metro stations Chandni Chowk and Red Fort are closest to this.

Figure: Parathe Wali Gali, one of the many busy lanes or Galis of Chandni Chowk market opposite red fort

Chandni Chowk today is full of wholesale markets and all kinds of shops. They are mostly grouped by types in narrow lanes or galis. Examples include Gali Parathewali, Gali Guliyan, Gali Ballimaran etc. Many of the shops sell clothes and jewellery, such as wedding apparal for men and women. Different galis are usually specialized in one types of shops, such as one for groceries, one for jewellery, one for food, one for books and so on.

Chandni Chowk is also famous for street food shops, many of which have become legends. Examples include Kareems for Biryani, Parathewali Gali for a number of Paratha shops, Shiv Mishtan Bhandar for sweets, Chatwallah for chaats, Old Famous Jalebi Wala in Dariba Kalan for jalebis and so on.

Chandni Chowk also has a number of Hawelis or medieval era mansions such as haweli of the famous Urdu poet Mirza Ghalib.

Figure: Digambar Jain Lal Mandir, ancient Jain temple in Chandni Chowk in Delhi, opposite the Red Fort

Figure: Gurudawara Sis Ganj in Chandni Chowk

Chandni Chowk also has a number of religious structures including mosques (Sunehri Masjid and Fatehpuri Masjid), Jain temple (Digambar Lal Jain Mandir), Sikh Gurudwara Sisganj Sahib, and Hindu temples like Gauri Shankar temple. Gurudwara Sisganj commemorates the place where the Sikh Guru Teg Bahadur was beheaded in the 18th century on orders of the Mughal emperor,

9.7 Mughal structures elsewhere in Delhi

Many other Mughal era structures are dotted around Delhi, including in the areas of the other historical cities. Jantar Mantar observatory is a notable Mughal era structure built by the Jaipur King and Mughal ally Jai Singh II and completed in 1724. It is located near the Connaught place.

Structures in Mehrauli area include Mughal emperor Bahadur Shah Zafar's palace. Near Nizamuddin also many Mughal area structures are existing, as it was considered auspicious to be buried close to the grave of the great Sufi saint Hazrat Nizamuddin Auliya.

9.8 Walks in Shahjahanabad

For the walk in the Red Fort Complex, one can take the metro to the Red Fort metro station, then cross the road to the Red Fort side and walk to the ticketing office and buy the ticket before proceeding towards the entrance to the Red Fort near the Lahori Gate. One can spend a long time exploring the Red Fort in a relaxed way, along with its different buildings and museums, as well as the adjoining Salimgarh Fort.

For a walk in Jama Masjid and Shahjahanabad, one can combine it with the Red Fort walk or treat it as a separate walk in itself. One can visit the Jama Masjid, its adjoining markets and climb the tower through its winding steps, after buying a ticket. One can see a clear view of old Delhi from the tower of the Jama masjid. Many delicious biryani and other shops are around the Jama masjid.

A stroll through crowded Chandni Chowk, with its mosques, temples and gurudwaras and eateries and shops in narrow galis is a treat in itself. One can spend the whole day exploring Chandni chowk and also some of the Hawelis including Mirza Ghalib's Haweli.

Nowadays there are also a few guided walking tours around Old Delhi and Chandni chowk. To join these guided tours, one can search google to register and pay online in advance and join the walking tours of old Delhi. For Red Fort, one may hire a registered qualified guide from near the entrance, usually they will have their badges displayed. A qualified guide can talk about the many stories around the Red Fort and about its history in detail.

9.9 Conclusion

In this chapter we have covered Shahjahanabad, or old Delhi and the various places one can visit in it, including the Red Fort, Jama masjid and markets like Chandni Chowk.

Chapter 10: New Delhi, historical city of Delhi

In this chapter we discuss the newest historical city of Delhi, which is New Delhi.

New Delhi is the British built city of Delhi, which also serves as the capital of India after Indian independence from British rule. It has many government buildings, national museums and administrative offices. The city was built over a few pre-existing villages and designed by the British architect Edwin Lutyens, in preparation for the British shifting the capital of India from Calcutta to Delhi in December of 1911.

Figure: Depiction of Edwin Lutyens overseeing the construction of Viceroy House in Delhi, now Rashtrapati Bhawan

10.1 How to get to historical sites in New Delhi

The nearest metro station is Central Secretariat, and the buildings are located around it. Distances between various sites in New Delhi can be relatively long, so it might be worthwhile hiring an auto rickshaw rather than walking. For Connaught place market, the nearest metro station is Rajiv Chowk.

10.2 Places to see in New Delhi: Kartavya Path (Formerly Rajpath)

New Delhi has a number of government offices, museums and historical sites built by the British. Some of the main British era historical sites are as follows:

- India Gate war memorial
- Raj Path (path connecting India Gate and Rashtrapati Bhavan)
- Rashtrapati Bhavan, formerly called Viceroy's house
- Central Secretariat
- Parliament House
- Teen Murti Bhavan
- Connaught Place
- Old Delhi Railway Station (located in Kashmere Gate, old Delhi but built by the British).
- St. Stephens College old building (located in old Delhi but built by the British).

The grand ceremonial boulevard connecting India Gate to Rashtrapati Bhavan was known as Rajpath ('King's Way') since the British era. In September 2022, it was renamed **Kartavya Path** ('Path of Duty') by the central government as part of a symbolic departure from colonial nomenclature. The avenue was simultaneously redeveloped with new pedestrian pathways, improved lighting consuming 80% less energy than before, enhanced water features, new parking areas, and more green spaces. It is now a significantly more pleasant and walkable public space.

Kartavya Path is the site of India's Republic Day parade every 26 January, one of the world's great ceremonial events, with military displays, cultural tableaux from every state, and a fly-past by the Indian Air Force.

Figure: Rashtrapati Bhavan or President's house in New Delhi, seen on top of Raisina Hill. Anupom sarmah, CC BY-SA 4.0 <https://creativecommons.org/licenses/by-sa/4.0>, via Wikimedia Commons

Figure: Depiction of Viceroy's House (now Rashtrapati Bhavan) during British times

10.3 Rashtrapati Bhavan

Formerly known as Viceroy's house and residence of the British Viceroy of India, this is the current residence of the President of India. It was designed by Edwin Lutyens and its construction was completed in 1929. It is located on the top of Raisina Hill, flanked by the secretariat buildings. Its architecture includes elements of classical Greek and Roman architecture along with some Indian elements. It has 340 rooms and a number of beautiful Mughal style gardens.

Some of the rooms and gardens in Rashtrapati Bhavan are open for viewing by members of the public, via advance booking on the Rashtrapati Bhavan website https://rb.nic.in/

Figure: India gate, the war memorial in New Delhi

10.4 India Gate

India Gate is a war memorial, built by the British to commemorate the 84000 soldiers of the British Indian army who died in the first world war. It is located on Rajpath. It can be freely viewed by the public. It also holds a living flame as Amar Jawan Jyoti or immortal flame to the unknown soldier, that was installed in 1972 after the Bangladesh liberation war. The Republic Day parade every year starts from India gate on January 26.

The **National War Memorial**, inaugurated in 2019, stands behind India Gate and commemorates India's soldiers who died post-independence. Admission is free. Note: The Amar Jawan Jyoti flame was merged with the National War Memorial flame in January 2022.

Figure: Secretariat building in New Delhi

10.5 Secretariat buildings

These are two identical buildings, North Block and South Block, on either side of Rashtrapati Bhavan on Raisina Hill. These were designed by British architect Sr Herbert Baker in Indo-Saracenic Revival architecture, and the construction was completed in 1927.

10.6 Parliament House or Sansad Bhavan

This is the place where the Parliament of India meets. It is located close to Rashtrapati Bhavan. It was designed by British architects Edwin Lutyens and Herbert Baker and completed in 1927. It is a circular building, containing within it three buildings which are the Lok Sabha, Rajya Sabha and a library. It is soon to be replaced with a new parliament house after the recent Central Vista redevelopment project is completed.

To visit the Parliament of India, one needs to apply for and receive a visitors pass from the security outside the parliament house. Visitors with a pass are also allowed to observe the parliament of India when it is in session. There is a parliament museum and a public gallery inside parliament house.

New Parliament Building — Inaugurated May 2023

India's new Parliament building, Sansad Bhavan, was inaugurated by Prime Minister Narendra Modi on **28 May 2023**, ahead of its August 2023 deadline. It was first used for official parliamentary business on **19 September 2023**.

Key facts:

- **Design:** Triangular in shape; designed by HCP Design Planning and Management (Ahmedabad-based architect Bimal Patel).
- **Construction:** Built by Tata Projects Ltd. at a cost of approximately ₹862 crore. Construction began October 2020 and took about 28 months.
- **Scale:** Built-up area of approximately 64,500 sq. metres across four floors.
- **Capacity:** The new Lok Sabha hall seats 888 MPs; the new Rajya Sabha hall seats 384 MPs. The building can accommodate up to 1,272 members for joint sessions — designed to handle the anticipated increase in parliamentary seats after delimitation.
- **Features:** Digital interface systems, acoustically designed chambers, a 6.5-metre-tall statue of India's national emblem (four Asiatic lions) on the facade.
- **Sengol:** A historical Tamil sceptre symbolising righteous governance, originally received at the transfer of power from the British in 1947, was installed in the new Lok Sabha chamber.

The old circular Parliament building (designed by Lutyens and Baker, completed 1927) will be preserved and converted into a museum open to the public. The two buildings stand side by side on Sansad Marg.

Central Vista Redevelopment Project

The new Parliament building is the centrepiece of the broader Central Vista Redevelopment Project, a comprehensive overhaul of India's central administrative area estimated to cost approximately ₹13,450 crore. Major components:

- **Central Vista Avenue (Kartavya Path):** Completed September 2022.
- **New Parliament Building:** Inaugurated May 2023.
- **Common Central Secretariat:** Ten interconnected buildings along Kartavya Path to house all 51 central government ministries in a single campus. As of early 2025, construction is approximately 22–38% complete depending on the building; full completion expected 2026–2027.
- **Executive Enclave:** Housing the Prime Minister's Office, Cabinet Secretariat, India House, and NSC Secretariat. Under construction by Larsen & Toubro.
- **North and South Blocks:** These iconic 1927 buildings will eventually be converted into publicly accessible museums celebrating India's history.

Figure: Parliament house in New Delhi. A.Savin, FAL, via Wikimedia Commons

Figure: Teen Murti Bhavan.

10.7 Teen Murti Bhavan

Teen Murti Bhavan is named after the three statues (teen murti) war memorial just outside the complex. Teen Murti Bhavan used to be the residence of the commander in chief of the British Indian army during British rule. After independence of India, the first Indian Prime Minister Jawaharlal Nehru used it as his residence. The building was completed in 1930.

Nowadays, it is converted into a museum dedicated to the life of Jawaharlal Nehru and contains an exhibition of his living quarters, the gifts he received etc. One can obtain a ticket for the same and view it. There is also a new museum called Pradhanmantri Sangrahalaya in an adjoining building, which highlights the life and times of all the prime ministers of India since independence. The same ticket is valid for both Teen Murti bhavan and Pradhanmantri Sangrahalaya.

Figure: Connaught Place in New Delhi

10.8 Connaught Place and Central Park

This is a series of white buildings in circular shape, located at the center of Delhi and contains a number of shops and business offices. It was built by the British and modelled after the Royal Crescent in Bath, United Kingdom. Its construction was completed in 1933.

It is built in a circular ring shape. Each of the buildings in it has two floors. The shops and offices are built on two rings, an outer ring and an inner ring, with radial roads in all directions from the inner ring. At the center of the Connaught place ring is a park called Central Park, with an underground market beneath the park called Palika Bazar.

Connaught place has a number of premium shops of many famous brands, as well as a number of restaurants. It also has an Indian version of Madame Tussaud's Wax Museum. There is a famous cinema called Regal in Connaught place, which serves as an important landmark.

Figure: Jaipur house, now part of the National Gallery of Modern Art or NGMA

10.9 Other British buildings in New Delhi

There are a number of other British era buildings in New Delhi. Examples include the Jaipur House, Delhi Gymkhana Club, Safdarjung Airport and so on.

Jaipur House, designed by Charles Blomfield in 1936 as the residence of the Maharaja of Jaipur, is now the National Gallery of Modern Art

(NGMA), and houses a number of important art collections. It can be visited by the public after buying a ticket.

Figure: St Stephens College Old Building in Kashmere Gate. Founded by the British in 1881 in Delhi.

Figure: St James church in Kashmere Gate

10.10 British era buildings in North Delhi

North Delhi has a number of British era buildings as well, particularly in Civil lines (Metro station: Civil Lines) and Kashmere gate (Metro station: Kashmere Gate). Civil lines is a quiet residential area in Delhi built by the British and where many British officials used to stay before independence. It is filled with wide streets, parks, British style bungalows and historical buildings.

Buildings in Kashmere gate include St Stephens College Old Building, St James Church and the Old Delhi Railway Station.

Figure: Old Delhi Railway Station building. The present building was constructed by the British in 1903. Lovedeepsingh, CC BY-SA 4.0 <https://creativecommons.org/licenses/by-sa/4.0>, via Wikimedia Commons

Figure: Maiden's Hotel in Civil Lines.

Figure: King George V statue in Coronation Park

British era buildings in Civil lines include Oberoi Maidens Hotel, Metcalfe's house, and Raj Niwas (official residence of the Lieutenant Governor of Delhi).

Coronation Park is an interesting Park further North from Kashmere gate, the nearest metro station being Majlis Park around 2 km away. It contains a lot of the British era statues such as that of King George

V, that were removed from other locations since the independence of India. It is a must visit for lovers of British Indian history.

10.11 Walks in New Delhi and Civil Lines

For walks in Connaught Place, one can take the metro to Rajeev Chowk and walk from there to see Regal Cinema, Central Park, Palika Bazaar and the shops and architecture of Connaught place.

For a walk in New Delhi, one can take the metro to Central Secretariat to view the many museums such as National Museum (near India gate), War Museum (near India Gate), Philately Museum (near Post Office) and National Gallery of Modern Art (near Jaipur House). One can also visit the Rashtrapati Bhavan and Parliament House, but prior registration and permission are needed for both before the actual visit.

For walks in Kashmere Gate and Civil Lines, one needs to get down at the metro station Kashmere Gate and Civil Lines respectively and walk from there.

For a walk in Coronation Park, one needs to get down in Majlis Park metro and take an autorickshaw or walk from there.

10.12 Conclusion

In this chapter we have discussed a few important British era buildings in New Delhi, the capital city of Delhi created by the British rulers.

Chapter 11: The many Delhi's

Delhi is not just one city—it is many. Layer upon layer, across millennia, Delhi has taken on multiple avatars: as a Vedic ritual centre, a Mauryan outpost, a spiritual crossroads of Jain and Buddhist traditions, a Rajput stronghold, a Mughal capital, a Sikh martyrdom site, a British colonial town, and finally, a modern megacity at the heart of India's political, intellectual, and economic life.

To understand Delhi fully, one must look beyond the seven historic cities typically counted in its medieval and early modern periods. This chapter explores the lesser-known but equally significant Delhis that have shaped the city's identity. These include ancient and spiritual Delhis, cultural and literary Delhis, refugee and post-Partition Delhis, and finally, the emerging Delhi of the National Capital Region (NCR).

This is the Delhi that stretches across time and space, across myth and monument, across empire and democracy. This is The Many Delhis.

11.1 Delhi in the Vedic Age: Kuru-Panchala and the Shatapatha Brahmana

Long before Delhi became the seat of emperors and sultans, it was part of one of the most influential cultural zones of early Vedic India—the region of Kuru-Panchalas.

The Shatapatha Brahmana, one of the most important Vedic texts associated with the Yajur Veda, frequently mentions the Kuru country, describing it as the heartland of Vedic ritualism and societal development. The Kurus were not just a tribe or kingdom—they were cultural innovators. It is in their land that the transition from tribal pastoralism to structured social and religious life took firm root.

The Kuru territory, which roughly corresponds to modern-day Delhi, Haryana, and western Uttar Pradesh, was known for:

- Standardizing Vedic sacrifices (yajnas),
- Codifying rituals that became central to Brahmanical orthodoxy,
- Nurturing a class of ritual specialists and philosophers who laid the foundation of Indian intellectual traditions.

By the period c. 800–600 BCE, regions like Delhi were no longer just pastoral lands but emerging centres of Vedic polity and thought. This connection explains why the *Mahabharata* places the capital of the Pandavas and Kauravas—Indraprastha—in what is now Purana Qila, at the heart of Delhi.

Figure: Ashoka pillar at Feroze Shah Kotla.

11.2 Ashokan Delhi: Mauryan Footprints in the Capital

By the 3rd century BCE, during the reign of Emperor Ashoka, Delhi had already gained strategic and symbolic importance. Though not a

Mauryan capital, it lay on a key administrative and trade route between the Gangetic plains and the northwest frontier of Ashoka's empire.

Evidence of Ashoka's reach into this region includes:

- Ashokan rock edicts and pillar inscriptions in areas around Delhi such as East of Kailash and Meerut.
- The Ashokan Pillar at Feroz Shah Kotla, brought from Topra in Haryana by Sultan Firoz Shah Tughlaq in the 14th century, still bearing Ashoka's edicts in Brahmi script.

These inscriptions place Delhi firmly within the Mauryan administrative network, used to spread Ashoka's message of *Dhamma* (ethical rule, compassion, and non-violence).

11.3 Buddhist Delhi: A Forgotten Chapter

Delhi's Buddhist past, though less visible today, was significant. Archaeological and textual references suggest that Indraprastha (identified with Purana Qila) remained inhabited through the Mauryan and post-Mauryan Buddhist eras.

Early Buddhist texts like the *Anguttara Nikaya* and *Jataka tales* mention the Kuru kingdom and its capital Indapatta (or Indapatta Nagar), believed to be ancient Delhi. The Kurus were known for their commitment to *dhamma*, qualities praised in Buddhist moral narratives.

Clues to continuous occupation include:

- Pottery shards, Northern Black Polished Ware (NBPW), and grey ware from Purana Qila excavations.
- Delhi's role as a crossroads of monastic travel, linking Mathura to Taxila.

Though no grand stupas remain, Delhi was part of early Buddhist India's cultural and ethical landscape.

Figure: Mahavir statue at Ahimsa Sthal near Qutub Minar

11.4 Jain Delhi: The Ancient Tradition in the Capital

Delhi has had a significant Jain presence since antiquity:

- In Mehrauli, Jain temples existed even before the Islamic conquests. Some pillars used in the Quwwat-ul-Islam mosque may have come from these structures.
- Lal Mandir (opposite Red Fort), built in 1656, is Delhi's oldest surviving Jain temple.
- Ahimsa Sthal near Qutub Minar, with a giant Mahavir statue, reflects Jain values of non-violence.

Jains played key roles in trade, administration, and philanthropy during Mughal and British rule.

11.5 Rajput Delhi: Tomars and Chauhans Before the Sultanate

The Rajput period laid the early urban foundations of Delhi:

- Tomar Dynasty: Anangpal Tomar is credited with founding Lal Kot in the 11th century and naming the city "Dhillika." His iron pillar (now at Qutub complex) marks this era.
- Chauhans of Ajmer: Prithviraj Chauhan, Anangpal's grandson, expanded the city into Qila Rai Pithora before being defeated in 1192 by Muhammad Ghori.

These rulers built Delhi's first baolis, temples, and fortifications, bridging ancient and medieval urbanism.

Figure: Gurudwara Sisganj in Chandni Chowk

11.6 Sikh Delhi: Martyrdom and Legacy

Delhi occupies a revered place in Sikh history. Some of the key events related to Sikhism were as follows:

- Guru Tegh Bahadur's martyrdom (1675) in Chandni Chowk, now commemorated by Gurudwara Sis Ganj Sahib.

- Banda Singh Bahadur challenged Mughal control after Guru Gobind Singh.

Some important historical Gurudwaras in Delhi include the following:

- Gurudwara Sis Ganj Sahib (Red Fort area)
- Gurudwara Bangla Sahib (Guru Har Krishan)
- Gurudwara Rakab Ganj Sahib (site of Guru Tegh Bahadur's cremation)

Sikh regiments also played a role in Delhi during the 1857 revolt and British era.

Figure: St James Church in Kashmere Gate

11.7 Christian Delhi: Colonial Faith and Community

British rule introduced Delhi's Christian institutions. Some of them are as follows:

- St. James' Church (1836), near Kashmere Gate, was the first major church.
- Numerous Catholic and Protestant churches arose in New Delhi after 1857.
- Delhi now has Syrian Christian and Anglo-Indian

communities as well.

11.8 Refugee Delhi: Post-Partition Migrations

In 1947, Delhi became a refuge for Partition survivors:

- Localities like Lajpat Nagar, Karol Bagh, Patel Nagar were established for Punjabi Hindu and Sikh refugees.
- Chittaranjan Park in New Delhi was set up for Bengali refugees from East Bengal.
- These communities reshaped Delhi's language, cuisine, economy, and cultural tone.

11.9 Cantonment Delhi: Military Township Legacy

- Built by the British, Delhi Cantonment was a separate military-administered township.
- It retains colonial-era bungalows, churches, and parade grounds.
- Even post-independence, it remains a distinct and protected military zone.

Figure: DLF Cybercity in Gurgaon. By Eatcha - Own work, CC BY-SA 4.0, https://commons.wikimedia.org/w/index.php?curid=77817432

Figure: Depiction of skyscrapers in Gurgaon

11.10 The Tenth City: Capital Delhi and the Rise of the NCR

Delhi has now evolved into a megacity and national capital region (NCR), including the following:

- Gurgaon (Gurugram): From farmland to Cyber City with Fortune 500 offices.
- Noida/Greater Noida: Planned townships with IT parks, Film City, and gated towers.
- Faridabad and Ghaziabad: Industrial suburbs turned residential hubs.

The Metro Rail system binds these together, forming a web of modern Delhi.

11.11 Conclusion

From Indraprastha to the NCR, Delhi is more than one city. It is simultaneously a timeline of Indian civilization, a canvas of faiths, languages, powers, and people, and a living organism which is always expanding, erasing, and remembering. It is, truly, the city of many Delhis.

Chapter 12: Practical Visitor's Guide

In this chapter we explore some suggested itineraries to explore Delhi, depending on one's time available.

12.1 Suggested Itinerary: Four Days in the Historical Cities of Delhi

Day 1: South Delhi — Mehrauli and Hauz Khas

1. Morning: Metro to Qutub Minar Station. Visit Mehrauli Archaeological Park (Jamali Kamali Mosque, baolis). Cross to Ahimsa Sthal Jain Temple.
2. Mid-morning: Buy ASI ticket and visit the Qutub Minar Group of Monuments.
3. Afternoon: Autorickshaw to Hauz Khas Village. Walk to Hauz Khas Fort Complex. Buy ASI ticket and visit the madrasa and tombs.
4. Late afternoon: Stroll Hauz Khas Village for coffee or a meal. Return to hotel via metro.

Day 2: Central Delhi — Sher Garh and Nizamuddin

1. Morning: Metro to Pragati Maidan. Walk or auto to Purana Qila. Buy ASI ticket, visit the Archaeological Museum, Qila-e-Kuhna Mosque, and Sher Mandal.
2. Afternoon: Walk or autorickshaw to Humayun's Tomb Complex. Buy ASI ticket. Visit the tomb and complex at leisure.
3. Late afternoon: Walk to Sunder Nursery (separate ticket) across the road.

4. Evening: Auto to Nizamuddin Dargah. Thursday evenings offer the best qawwali experience.

Day 3: Old Delhi — Shahjahanabad

1. Morning: Metro to Red Fort Station. Buy ASI ticket and spend the morning at the Red Fort Complex and Salimgarh Fort. Consider hiring a licensed guide at the entrance.
2. Noon: Cross the road to Jama Masjid. Explore the mosque and climb the minaret for views of Old Delhi.
3. Afternoon: Stroll through Chandni Chowk and its galis. Sample street food — paratha, chaat, jalebi.
4. Late afternoon: Visit Digambar Lal Jain Mandir and Gurudwara Sis Ganj Sahib.

Day 4: New Delhi — Kartavya Path and Lutyens' Delhi

1. Morning: Metro to Central Secretariat. Walk Kartavya Path from India Gate towards Rashtrapati Bhavan. Visit the National War Memorial.
2. Mid-morning: Visit the area around the new Parliament building. View the old and new Sansad Bhavan side by side.
3. Afternoon: Metro to Rajiv Chowk (Connaught Place). Explore the circular markets, Central Park, and the Palika Bazaar underground market.
4. Late afternoon: Optional visit to Jantar Mantar (ASI ticket, very near Connaught Place).

12.2 Delhi Metro Quick Reference Table

Historical Site / Area	Nearest Metro Station	Line (Colour)
Qila Rai Pithora	Saket	Yellow
Qutub Minar / Mehrauli	Qutub Minar	Yellow
Hauz Khas / Siri Fort	Hauz Khas	Yellow
Tughlaqabad Fort	Tughlaqabad	Violet
Jahanpanah (Bijay Mandal)	Hauz Khas	Yellow
Feroze Shah Kotla Fort	ITO / Delhi Gate	Violet
Purana Qila	Pragati Maidan	Blue
Humayun's Tomb / Nizamuddin	Jangpura	Pink
Lodi Gardens	Jor Bagh / Khan Market	Yellow
Red Fort / Salimgarh	Red Fort	Violet
Jama Masjid	Jama Masjid	Violet
Chandni Chowk	Chandni Chowk	Yellow
India Gate / Kartavya Path	Central Secretariat	Yellow/ Violet
New & Old Parliament	Central Secretariat	Yellow/ Violet
Connaught Place / Jantar Mantar	Rajiv Chowk	Yellow/Blue
Kashmere Gate / Civil Lines	Kashmere Gate / Civil Lines	Yellow
Coronation Park	Majlis Park	Pink

12.3 Safety and Etiquette Tips

- Use only licensed taxis and apps (Ola, Uber) for rides, or prepaid autorickshaws.
- Be cautious of touts near popular monuments offering unofficial guides or redirecting you to shops.

- At mosques and dargahs, remove footwear. At gurudwaras, cover your head.
- Carry small denomination notes (₹10, 20, 50) for autorickshaws, shoe-keepers, and tips.
- The metro has separate women-only coaches (the first coach of every train).
- Be respectful when photographing locals — always ask for permission.

12.4 Useful Websites

- Delhi Metro: www.delhimetrorail.com[1]
- ASI Ticketing: https://asi.payumoney.com/
- ASI information: www.asi.nic.in[2]
- Rashtrapati Bhavan visits: https://rb.nic.in/
- Delhi Tourism (HOHO bus etc.): www.delhitourism.gov.in[3]

---

1. http://www.delhimetrorail.com

2. http://www.asi.nic.in

3. http://www.delhitourism.gov.in

Chapter 13: Conclusion

In the previous chapters of this book, we have discussed multiple historical cities in Delhi. For each of the cities, we have briefly discussed the historical background, the main sites or buildings in that city, how to get there using Delhi metro and how to plan a walk in that area.

Delhi is indeed one of the amazing cities of India, being the site of so many political upheavals and changes of rulers and ruling dynasties. For hundreds of years, whoever has ruled Delhi has also ruled over most of India. Each gali, each mohalla, each haveli, each road of this city has probably got some history behind it. Even now, being the current national capital of India, history is being made in this city and it is expanding like never before. That is why it is useful to have some appreciation of its historical cities, both of residents of Delhi as well as visitors.

It is hoped that this book will help the reader a little in this direction.

Glossary of Key Terms

ASI: Archaeological Survey of India — the government body responsible for the protection and maintenance of India's archaeological heritage and historical monuments.

Baoli: A step well — a subterranean structure with steps leading down to water, used for water storage and as a social gathering space. Examples include Rajon ki Baoli and Gandhak ki Baoli in Mehrauli.

Charbagh: A Persian-style formal garden divided into four quadrants by water channels. Humayun's Tomb garden is a famous example.

Chattri: An elevated, dome-shaped pavilion used as a decorative element in Mughal and Rajput architecture. Found commonly atop tombs and gateways.

Dargah: The shrine or tomb of a Sufi saint, which often becomes a place of pilgrimage and worship. Sheikh Nizamuddin Auliya's dargah is one of the most important in India.

Darwaza: Gateway or door. Historical forts and cities often have multiple named darwazas. Examples: Lahori Darwaza (Red Fort), Bada Darwaza (Purana Qila).

Diwan-e-Aam: Hall of Public Audience — where the Mughal emperor met ordinary subjects and heard public petitions and grievances.

Diwan-e-Khas: Hall of Private Audience — where the Mughal emperor received important guests and state officials. Often more richly decorated than the Diwan-e-Aam.

DMRC: Delhi Metro Rail Corporation — the agency that builds and operates the Delhi Metro.

Gali / Galli: A narrow lane or alley, typical of the old quarters of Delhi. Chandni Chowk has many famous galis.

Gumbad: A dome. The term is often used in the name of domed structures, e.g., Bada Gumbad (Large Dome) in Lodi Gardens.

Hammam: A bath house or bathing chamber in a Mughal palace. The Red Fort has a well-known hammam.

Haveli: A large, traditional townhouse or mansion, typically with an interior courtyard. Many notable havelis are found in Chandni Chowk and Old Delhi.

Jaali: Intricately perforated stone or marble lattice screens used in Mughal architecture for privacy, ventilation, and decoration. Notable examples at Humayun's Tomb.

Madrasa: An Islamic school or seminary for religious education. Many are associated with historical mosques in Delhi.

Minaret: A tall slender tower attached to or beside a mosque, from which the call to prayer is made. The Qutub Minar is a famous minaret.

NCR: National Capital Region — the greater metropolitan area of Delhi, including the city itself plus parts of Haryana, Uttar Pradesh, and Rajasthan.

Qawwali: Devotional Sufi music performed at dargahs, often on Thursday evenings. The Nizamuddin Dargah is one of the best places in India to experience it.

Qila: Fort or citadel. Many historical cities in Delhi are centred on a qila.

Sultanate: The Delhi Sultanate (1206–1526) — a succession of five Muslim dynasties (Slave/Mamluk, Khalji, Tughlaq, Sayyid, Lodi) that ruled Delhi before the Mughals.

UNESCO World Heritage Site: A site recognised by UNESCO as being of outstanding universal value. Delhi has three: the Red Fort Complex, Humayun's Tomb, and the Qutub Minar Complex.

Yamuna: The river on whose banks Delhi stands. Many of Delhi's historical cities were built along or near its banks.

About the authors

Siva Prasad Bose is an author of introductory guidebooks on aspects of Indian laws. He is currently retired after many years of service as an electrical engineer in Uttar Pradesh Power Corporation Limited. He received his engineering degree from Jadavpur University, Kolkata and has a law degree from Meerut University, Meerut and a BSc from MMH College, Ghaziabad. His interests lie in the fields of family law, civil law, law of contracts, and areas of law related to power electricity related issues. He lives in Delhi.

Joy Bose is a data scientist by profession.

Other Books by Siva Prasad Bose

Introduction to Wills and Probate

Senior Citizens Abuse in India

Introduction to Negotiable Instruments

Introduction to Marriage Laws in India

Neighbor Problems in India and what to do about them

Delays in Court Cases in India

Self-Publish Books and E-Books in India

Introduction to Patents and Patent Law in India

Introduction to Property Law in India

Did you love *Historical Cities of Delhi: Walks Using the Delhi Metro*?
Then you should read *A Walk in Chittaranjan Park*[1] by Siva Prasad
Bose and Joy Bose!

[2]

Chittaranjan Park or CR park is a residential colony in South Delhi, bordered by Greater Kailash 1 and 2 and located close to areas such as Nehru place, Alaknanda, Kalkaji and Govindpuri. It is sometimes called "Little Kolkata" because of the Kolkata style street food, Bengali culture and festivals celebrated here.

Previously called EPDP Colony or East Pakistan Displaced Persons Colony and Purbachal, CR Park is a Bengali dominated colony that was originally developed to house refugees of partition from East Bengal, but has recently become more diverse. It is a cultural treat famous for its celebration of Durga Puja, Bengali snacks and sweets.

---

1. https://books2read.com/u/bMYWXv

2. https://books2read.com/u/bMYWXv

In this book we discuss the famous landmarks and festivals in CR Park. This is intended to be partly a travel guide for those who want to experience this microcosm of Bengali culture in New Delhi.

Our own Bose family has been resident in Delhi for a very long time, originally residing in Kashmere Gate and later moving to CR Park.

About the Author

Siva Prasad Bose is an electrical engineer by profession. He is currently retired after many years of service in Uttar Pradesh Power Corporation Limited. He received his engineering degree from Jadavpur University, Kolkata and has a law degree from Meerut University, Meerut. His interests lie in the fields of family law, civil law, law of contracts, and any areas of law related to power electricity related issues.

Read more at https://sivaprasadbose.wordpress.com/.